From the bonnie banks of Loch Lomond

to
Birmingham
By James L Hamilton and Grace Miles

The story of a brother and sister's journey through life

Part 1. Our childhood years in Scotland

This book has previously been published as an ebook on Amazon Kindle in two parts which have been combined for this paperback book

Foreword

Grace and I were born in Scotland in the 1940s of an English mother and Scottish Father.
I think for our parents, these were not easy times after the years of war and now the slow return to something near to normal life, still with shortages, rationing and low wages.
However, our recollections are of a happy home where there was love, we had fun and our parents did their best for us.
This is our story as we both remember it now after all these years.
Grace and I have written our accounts separately and not conferred which becomes apparent when you read, as we often remember different things or the same things differently.

Prologue

Loch Lomond is a wonderful place to visit with stunning scenery and places of interest.
You could say we were very privileged to have been born and brought up there in our early years and certainly we have many memories of exciting things we did and the many places we enjoyed visiting. However, although we lived on the doorstep of Loch Lomond as you will read, our memories are of being brought up on a council estate just south of the Loch, in a loving happy home, with having many friends who we had lots of fun and adventures with.
We did I think seem to take advantage of the locality more that others around us, I wonder however if that had something to do with having an English mother, (probably rare in Scotland in those days) who seemed to enjoy taking us for days out and doing lots of things with us. In later life I have returned for visits with my wife and then with our children when they were young where we had some very happy family holidays. While there, I have often thought how lovely it was to have been born and raised in our early years in such a wonderful place. This is our story.

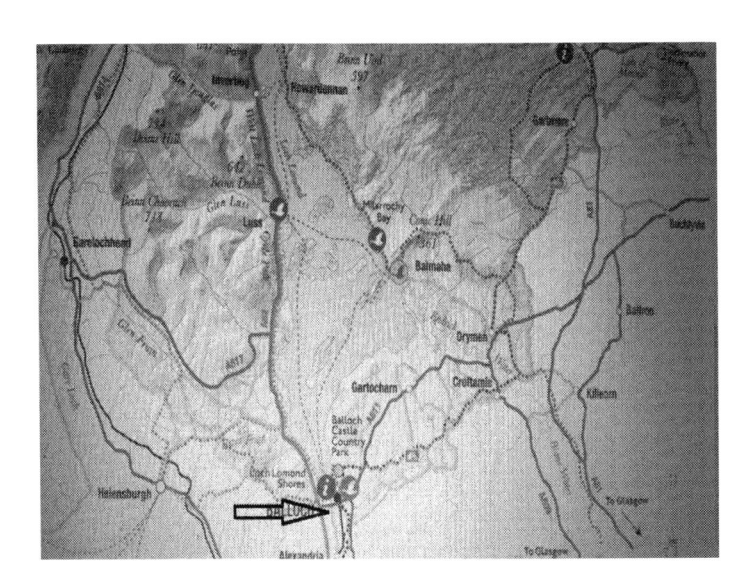

Our beginnings

Grace's first recollections

War Baby

I was born in 1942 during the second World War, to a working class couple called James and Minnie Hamilton. James and Minnie were Christians and had met at a Christian conference in Herne Bay. James was Scottish and lived in Glasgow, and Minnie lived in Birmingham with her family – 3 sisters and 1 brother - Lottie, Dolly, Jack, and Mary.

Granny & Grandad and children

I suppose it was difficult for James and Minnie to get together very often during the war with them living so far apart, but they did eventually get married and Minnie left her family to live in Scotland.

Mum and Dad's Wedding

By then James had moved 20 miles north of Glasgow to Jamestown, not far from Loch Lomond. He was excused being called up for the war because he had a 'Reserved Occupation' at the Royal Naval Torpedo factory in Alexandria.

Later, after the war ended, my Dad continued to work at the factory which had been turned into an engineering company – though it continued to be known by the locals as 'The Torpedo Factory'.

The Royal Naval Torpedo Factory   (Cars were not like this when I was

The Village of Jamestown

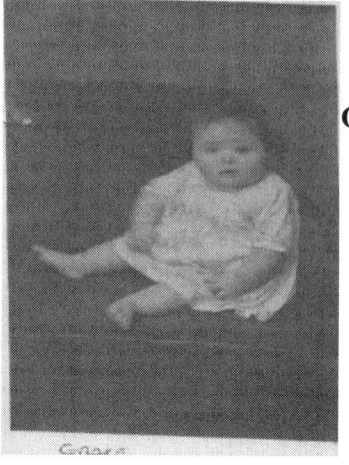

Grace – their first born.

I was born on the 17th July 1942, 3 years before the end of World War 2. I have only one recollection of the war. I clearly remember wondering why all our windows were blacked out by heavy blinds which were drawn as soon as it became dusk. I lifted the corner of a blind one evening, and was shouted at for doing so! Every household during the war were ordered to black out their windows to prevent the bombers finding lights to target for their bombing raids at night!

I don't think we had the terrible bombing that London, Birmingham and Coventry had – I have no memory of seeing bombed-out houses, or having to rush down our air raid shelter. However, in case we did have bombing raids by the Germans, Mum and Dad had to dig a big hole in the garden and were issued with a large semi circular sheet of corrugated iron which was our air raid shelter. It's surprising that we didn't have more bombing really, because the Torpedo Factory was just down the road, and the Royal Navy submarine base was on the West Coast of Scotland also.

After the end of the war life improved, though rationing continued until 1950 to enable the country to get back on its feet. I remember seeing the ration book with dated coupons – only a small amount of meat was able to be bought each week, and we had to produce our coupon to enable this to be bought. Meat was mostly offal – liver, kidney, tripe (which none of us liked), mince, ox tongue or ox tail. We couldn't be fussy, though, it was that or nothing! We also ate lots of dried egg, and spam!

During the war most men were called up for service and the married women looked after their families, meaning that many families were split up, and the menfolk who were called up were absent for months at a time. Single women or those who had no children volunteered for the Land Army, working on farms, keeping the food chain running, or worked in factories producing armaments.

Many factories were very understaffed, so we were rationed for clothes and shoes also– it was usually only 1 pair of shoes and sandals a year, and 1 winter coat per year. I can still remember how exciting it was to get a new coat or pair of shoes!!

There was a real community spirit in our road on this council estate. Everyone was in the same boat – all were struggling to make ends meet and sympathised and helped each other out when help was needed. No one seemed to lock their doors when they went out, perhaps because there were no valuables to steal!!

I remember my mum telling me how when about 4 years old I went out to play with my friends in the road and some time later she found I was missing. Going from door to door asking if anyone had seen me, I was eventually discovered sitting in the home of one of our neighbours who had gone shopping. I had apparently opened their door, gone into their house and was sat in their lounge eating one of their apples!! Oops!

It was safe to play outdoors in the street during the whole of my childhood. There were very few cars around, just the occasional van selling bread or fish, or the milkman's horse and cart. Most men went to work on their bikes, or by bus.

Me and my little brother – Jimmy

Arrival of Brother Jimmy and schooldays

When I was 4 my brother Jimmy was born, and we then applied for an exchange to a bigger council maisonette round the corner. However, we weren't there long and again moved to a council prefab in Tullichewan, - 13, Broomley Crescent; a short distance away.

View from our prefab's back garden.

We loved our prefab which was very compact. Although small, it was detached and had 2 bedrooms, a lounge, kitchen and bathroom. The kitchen had a built in cooker, boiler for washing clothes, and fridge. So our furniture consisted of 1 table and 4 chairs, 3 piece suite, organ, sideboard, radiogram, 2 single beds and a double bed. Our tiny garden was filled mostly with a greenhouse so my Dad could grow peas, marrows, carrots, lettuces and tomatoes. Potatoes were outside in the borders surrounding the tiny lawn.
We were very happy there. It was an idyllic place to grow up in as we were just 20 minutes walk from Loch Lomond, our favourite place to spend Saturdays, and most of our time during the summer holidays.

****

Jimmy's recollections

I started life at the early age of 0, as most people do, on 22/11/1946. I have no recollection of the occasion of course. The address of my birth is 48 Engels Street, Alexandria, Dunbartonshire, Scotland. Shortly after this event, my family moved to Hardie Street which was a short distance away on the same council estate.

After two years we moved again, that is my mum, dad and sister who was already four years old when I was born. We moved just few hundred yards, to the other side of Luss Road, the main road then that went from Glasgow to Loch Lomond.

Our move this time was to a new scheme (estate in English) of prefabricated bungalows known more widely as 'prefabs'. Our new address was 13 Broomley Crescent, Tullichewan. (Pronounced Tulliquewen), Alexandria, Dunbartonshire, Scotland.

.

This picture which I have found on the internet is of Bannachra Crescent, it ran parallel to our road on the back of our prefab and was taken in 1953 when we were all celebrating Queen Elizabeth's coronation. I was seven years old, but I don't remember anyone in this photo. My dads' brother, Uncle Robert lived on this road with his lovely wife, Auntie Minnie.

We probably would think it to be sad to be living in a prefab bungalow today, but in those days just after the war when there was a housing shortage, amongst many other things, I suspect you felt quite well off and privileged to be renting one. Certainly, my memories of living there were good ones.

The scheme had been built on the site of an army camp which had been set up during world war two in the grounds of Tullichewan Castle which was nestled in the hillside behind our house. This beautiful building was clearly visible from our back garden.

There were still a few nissen huts at the top our road, left by the army when they left, which had been taken over by people who had nowhere to live at the end of the war.

Mum and Dad

My father, James Hutton Smith Hamilton, was born and raised in Glasgow to James Hamilton and Isabella Hamilton, in November 1893. He had two brothers and a sister, George, Robert and Kate, I never got to meet my grandparents on dads side, so I presume they had already passed away when I was born.

Our mother, Minnie Cecilia Ann Lawrence, was from Birmingham, born February 1906, she had three sisters and a brother. They had lived with their mother and father, Minnie and Ernest Lawrence, in the Solihull district. I can only remember granny and granddad being old, but I understand that Granddad had worked in a factory where he straightened wire which was made into nails I think. Granny stayed at home and was a housewife which was the norm in those days.

I know very little of mum's childhood days but when the Lawrence children were in there twenties, there was a large Christian tent crusade in Birmingham run by George Jeffrey. It drew thousands of Birmingham folk each night, she told us many were healed of various ailments and it's said 10,000 were converted to the Christian faith. Among them were all the Lawrence children. Our mother often related how, along with thousands of others, they were all baptised in local swimming baths afterwards. She subsequently joined the Pentecostal Church where she became a committed member and involved in Sunday school work and was a gifted story teller to children. She made up many of her own stories.

When she was in her thirties, she went to a Christian convention in North Wales. It was here that she met a man from Glasgow who was to become her future husband. So it was that Minnie Cecilia Ann Lawrence married James Hutton Smith Hamilton in 1939 at the age of 33.

After they were married my mum moved to live in Scotland with dad and thus, Gracie and Jimmy (me) were born, Scottish but with an English mother.

Nought to nine

Its hard to say at what age memories start to be recorded, I think my earliest must be at a time when rationing was still in force after the war and the food we ate in those days was a bit sparse and plain, sometimes for tea we would have bread and butter with sugar lightly sprinkled on it and it felt like you were eating a sandwich with sand in it, (I wonder if that's where the name comes from), except it was sweeter than sand. We had very few treats at this time but one I remember was we had was a small amount of shredded coconut given us in a brown paper bag, a bit chewy but still enjoyable. I can also remember around this time, on being left alone in the kitchen for a while, opening the cupboard door under the sink and discovering to my delight a brown paper bag with white flakes in it which I immediately started to eat. I don't remember anything of the taste but it caused quite an upset for my mum and dad, they were really worried about me and I felt quite guilty that I had done something really bad. Fortunately, I didn't seem to have come to any harm whatever it was.

After that my earliest memories are of having best friends, Ian and Ian who lived in the same road and the games we played together and with other boys and girls who lived around us. My best girl friend was Violet. Her older sister, Margaret, was best friend to Gracie, they lived over the road from us.

We all played the usual games in the road, froggy froggy let me cross your water, skipping with a long washing line with everyone joining in, hide and seek, hop scotch (drawn on the pavement with chalk) and so on and would often be allowed to continue playing out in the summers till quite late in the evening. No one owned a car then on our estate and there were never any cars coming up our road so we were quite safe, the only traffic was the rag and bone man with his horse and cart, shouting as he passed, 'rags, old rags', and the milk man with his horse and cart and later in his Bedford van early each morning. He would sometimes give a few of us lads a ride round the roads of our scheme on a Saturday morning and we would help him with his deliveries, the ice-cream van with its loud honking horn, (very important to the Scots) and the Corona truck delivering lemonade in glass bottles, which on the next delivery, a deposit of 2d was paid back to you for their return. I think the Corona man only went to a few houses in our road, most couldn't afford it.

There was only one television that we ever new of on the estate during the time we lived there, so radio and gramophone were the only entertainment we had which we always listened to during the day and in the evenings. I can remember listening to workers playtime and the Goon show around lunch time. I remember to this day how Harry Secombe made the discovery that the sun was on fire and called out the fire brigade and Peter sellers promptly put it out, how I laughed. On the gramophone, we played 'Carolina Moon keep shinning' and 'Thou art the everlasting Word' by a Welsh male voice choir, must have listened to them a lot to have such a vivid memory.

The children's hour at five o'clock had exciting stories and plays. This had a definite influence on some of the games we played. There must have been an adventure story about escaping from a prison camp because I decided with my friends Ian and Ian, that we would dig a tunnel under the wire fence at the side of our house between front and back gardens, and make our escape. We had made good progress until the camp commander (my mother) discovered our hole and was concerned that the foundations of the house, whatever they were, could be damaged. We were told in no uncertain terms we would have to fill it in, much to our disappointment.

Before filling it in though, Ian and I thought we would have a joke on the other Ian. I found some strips of spring steel off an old bedstead, which we laid across the hole and covered these lightly with soil and then brought the other Ian in to play steam roller over it to firm it down. It was a good laugh for us as we watched our friend slowly sinking down deeper and deeper into the hole. I don't think he minded, he had fun and enjoyed the joke.

At the back of our estate was a rough field which was in between us and the hill that the castle was set in. This provided hours of fun for all us kids, free from all adult constraints, here we could build dens, climb trees, have imaginary adventures. One time we must have been listening to a spy story on the wireless and a few of us lads went and hid in the field after tea pretending to be working for MI5 looking for spies. As we lay in our hideout we noticed a man walking through the field and one of the lads who we didn't know very well, started shouting at him saying we knew who he was but then he used some bad words which surprised the rest of us. Unfortunately it was a still evening and his voice could be heard over much of the estate so when we went home he found his mother waiting for him in the street with a face like thunder. We gathered he was in a lot of trouble.

The field had a little stream (or 'burn' in Scottish), which we dammed, jumped over and splashed through. We played there a lot. Behind that, partway up the hill was the old Tullichewan castle. I don't know if it was inhabited then, but it had glass in the windows and looked like someone could have been living there

Easter

I don't have any remembrance of having chocolate Easter eggs in Scotland in those days, maybe they appeared at a later time. What we did though was hard boil some eggs, paint faces onto them and then dad would take us all on the bus down to Alexandria where we would walk out of the town, up the hill to the reservoir, where there was some lovely views of the town and valley in which it was situated.

On the sides of the reservoir were some nice grassy banks and here we followed the strange custom of rolling our eggs down the hill. I think we also quite enjoyed rolling ourselves down the hill as well. After a picnic and a few more games, we would pack up and start our walk back down to the town.

Tullichewan Castle

The driveway up to the castle

Summer

At weekends in the summer, weather permitting, my mum, dad, me and Gracie, would go for a walk across the field at the back of the estate, up to Tullichewan castle, (pronounced Tulliquwen), then follow the lane which went along in front of it and led us round the back of Alexandria hospital and down the side of Christie park into Alexandria town and then back along the main street to our home, I think it must have been a fair walk because my dad would often carry me on his shoulders for some of the way. Christie Park was and is still a lovely park but I don't ever remember going into it, we had another park that was closer to us which had swings. Maybe that was the reason we never went to Christie Park.

Christie Park

Then besides all of these wonderful places to play, we had Loch Lomond which was about a twenty minute walk.
In the summer, mum would often take us and a few of our friends down to Balloch.

From our scheme we would walk down the Luss Road, turning right onto Balloch Road where there was a hotel, a large white building on the right which is still there today, not sure what it is now. Further down that road on the left was a silk factory with its tall chimneys, all gone now. At the bottom of the road was the railway station on the left side of the road. It had a level crossing with wooden gates which closed the road off every time a train came steaming through. After stopping in Balloch station, the train would continue up to the last station on the line which was right on the pier on Loch Lomond. In those days the trains would come here, full of day trippers from Glasgow, to connect with the steamers that would take them for a great day out, cruising all the way up Loch.

There was a narrow road connecting Balloch to the most southerly shore of Loch Lomond. We would often walk this road which took you along the side of the railway tracks where you could see the steam trains coming and going. About half way down was a turn table in the tracks, it was amazing to see an engine be driven onto the it and the driver and fireman come down from their engines and get hold of this huge steaming machine and pull it round by hand to face the other way and then set off on their return journey to Glasgow, this was pure magic for us young lads.

On the south shore of Loch Lomond at the end of this road was a small sandy beach. At some time I seem to remember there had been a wooden pier jutting out from this shore, there are just the stumps protruding from the water now. The main pier stood to the right of this, from where steamers departed which is the same one in use today.
The beach was a great place to paddle and play, I don't remember swimming there though, instead we would cross the bridge over the river Leven and go up a path in Balloch Park along side the river. The river Leven from the bridge up to the Loch in those days was jam packed full of motor launches and house boats moored along the sides of the rivers where presumably some people lived, but many of them, in my recollection, were looking petty old and shabby even in those days.
From a jetty there by the bridge you could catch one of Sweenies motor launches which would take you on a short cruise on the Loch. They are still operating today, but have modern larger boats now.
In the summer, mum would take us to a sheltered spot on the river where there was a gap between the boats that were moored there. Here was a safe little sandy bay, set back from the current of the river where we could swim, have fun and have our picnic. I think I fancied myself as a deep sea diver on one occasion, swimming down to the bottom of the riverbed, complete with my buoyancy aid. In reality, I must have been paddling along on the surface with my head submerged. Finally, when running out of air and needing to surface quickly, I reached out and grasped the nearest thing possible which happened to be a girl who was standing nearby, who looked at me in astonishment, wondering what on earth I was doing.

The river Leven, Baloch.

I can only remember the summers being hot and sunny but judging by our holidays we have taken in the area later in life, it must have rained quite a lot.
Our summers were great times, playing out with our friends in the street or in our back garden and where me and Grace sometimes had our own little picnics inviting some of our friends or even just our cat and canary (in its cage).
We got on well with lots of the kids on the estate but there were a few of a rougher sort that you had to be careful with. One time I had been given a trick ring which you put on your finger and it could squirt water from a hidden little rubber container in the palm of your hand, I unwisely showed this to a lad who was a bit of a bully, when he had water shot into his eyes he was not at all amused and he grabbed hold of me and threw me against the fence which we were standing near. I went home shaken and crying expecting my mum to go out and give the boy a good telling off but instead it was me that got told I had been

silly to play nasty tricks on people and I should learn not to do this kind of thing. I think it was a lesson I did learn!! We had bonfire night in Scotland. I don't ever remember any bonfires but we did have a few small fireworks and maybe a rocket which my dad let off in our back garden. They were always really exciting for us, the traffic signals which burned with different colours, the Roman candle, the Catharine wheel, which always got stuck and had to be knocked to get it going again, probably they were pretty tame in comparison to fireworks today but we thought they were great. We did however have one called a 'jumping jack' which is no longer available . It was like a little worm tied up in an 'm' shape. When lit, it made a loud bang followed by about six more. Only thing was that each time there was a bang it jumped up in the air and landed in a different place, you didn't know where it would land, so you had to run away to a safe distance once lit. Well, one of my friends got hold of one of these and lit it in the middle of the road. We ran off and watched in awe as it jumped all over the place with each crack but wouldn't you just know it, on the last but one jump, it landed on the windowsill of our next door neighbours house, an old lady who lived by herself whom we tended to try to avoid. Bang, it went as it flew off from her window, fortunately not causing any damage. We ran for our lives and hid up the side of our house, peeping round to see her come to the front door to see who the culprits were. She never found out who did it and I don't think we ever did that again.

Winter

Winters were pretty cold with lots of rain probably and sometimes snow. When it did snow, we had an old wooden sledge which we would take up to some fields on the hill at the back of our house, here there was a very long field which was nicknamed 'the half mile' which the very brave would sledge down at great speed. I can't remember ever being brave enough to go the full distance, maybe Grace did though!?

One winter, I got the measles or something and had to sleep in the lounge where it was warmer. I could see out of the window that it was snowing heavily and while it was exciting to watch it, I was disappointed too that I would not be able to play out in it.

I seem to remember that we often suffered with cold feet and had to hang our socks on the radiators at school to try and get them warm again

Christmas

At Christmas, as was the experience of most kids in those days, we would hang our socks at the end of the bed and excitedly wake up on Christmas day morning to find Father Christmas had filled them with nuts, tangerines and various fruits, which we thought was wonderful. Maybe we got a comic annual as well, I can remember having Rupert Bear and a very Scottish one, 'Oor Willie' which my dad used to read to me. One year though, I remember my mum taking me to the toy shop in Alexandria several weeks before Christmas and being told to choose a toy for Father Christmas to bring to me. The one I chose was a little clockwork train going round on landscape which was made of tin and a helicopter on a small wire arm which hovered round over the top of the train. I was very excited to be getting it but on Christmas day, when I opened the present though, it was different from what I had chosen, this one was a clockwork train and few little trucks which went round in a circle on a small track which you had to lay out

on the floor. I was initially a bit disappointed with this as it wasn't what I had asked father Christmas for and was further confused when my mum asked at the shop why I had got the wrong train and they explained that they had run out of the one I had asked for, somehow though, it didn't seem to shake my confidence in Santa.
On another Christmas, I can remember getting a tin toy American police car which had a siren which wailed when you pushed it forward. I had many happy hours playing with it which must have driven my mum mad.

Our house

Our prefabricated bungalow, like all the others on the scheme, was made I think of asbestos walls and roof. No one new in those days that asbestos was dangerous, but it doesn't seemed to have affected us thankfully.
Inside, it had two bedrooms of reasonable size, Grace and I shared the back one which had two single beds, mum and dad had the front. There was a central hallway which we called 'the lobby' and was big enough to keep things in like bikes and prams etc. In the lobby was the front door and the doors to the bedrooms, toilet and bathroom and sitting room. Through the sitting room was the kitchen on the back of the house again. In our sitting room, we had some brown armchairs, maybe made of imitation leather, a radiogram and our bellows operated organ which you peddled with you feet. I liked to play it with one finger. Our fireplace was a coal burning fire with a glass door, which I assume was the only source of heat in the house. In the kitchen we had what we would now consider to be an old style cooker, sink and cupboards and a table and chairs where we had our meals. All the cupboards and wardrobes throughout the home were conveniently inbuilt to the

prefab and made of metal and painted cream.
The back door was on the side of the house leading into the kitchen, this was the door we used mostly when we were going out to play and it was always unlocked.

Dad

I don't know much about my dads early years or about his parents, only that he was bald from a young age; my mum said it was because his parents hadn't washed his hair properly, not sure if she was right there though.
When mum and dad were first married, I believe they enjoyed going out riding bikes all round the beautiful countryside where we lived and also walking, Mum said they even climbed Ben Lomond which is quite a hike at 3196 feet high

Ben Lomond

I can faintly remember we also went on a walk up a track on the hill behind our home which is called 'Stoneymollan', it took you right over the top of the hill and all the way to Cardross on the Clyde. There are some amazing views of Loch Lomond from the top. Once over to the other side we got a bus or train to go back home. Looking at it on the map now it looks an awful long way and the hill is pretty high, so it must have been a very full day.

My dad worked in the RNTF, Royal Navy Torpedo Factory. An impressive building a bit less than a mile away which he cycled to each day.

It had been a car factory originally, opened in 1906, producing Argyll cars, then, after the demise of the company in 1926 it had been used for various things including the production of munitions in the First World War.

In 1939 at the outbreak of war, it was taken over by the Royal Navy and my dad worked there as a turner, presumably making parts for torpedo's.

The only story I know of the war years, told to us by mum when we were older was that a German plane flew over Alexandria one day and the gunners, who were situated on the factory roof, opened fire on it, which they were under strict instruction not to do and were roundly told off afterwards because it would reveal the existence and position of the factory to them. Fortunately for them they managed to hit it and it crashed in the mountains not far away and the factory remained a secret.

Our Dad was a gentle quite and loving man from what I remember. Before setting off for work each morning, he would come into our bedroom and lick open Gracie's and my eyes to help us wake up so he could say goodbye to us, then after a kiss he would set off on his cycle to the factory about half a mile away and go in through the well guarded gates at the far end of the building. Even after the war had ended, they still continued for some years to make torpedoes. I often walked past the works with my mum on our way down to the shops in Alexandria and would look at the large darkened windows at the front, and see the sentries at the gates and wish I could see what was going on in there.

Much later on in life, after I got married, my wife and I went on holiday to Loch Lomond and we were delighted to find the building had now been converted into a retail outlet and we were able to go in and see round some of it. This picture is of the marble staircase at the main entrance and the corridor to the left at the top led to the dinning rooms for the workers. It was a wonderful experience for me to have climbed those stairs and wondered how often my dad had walked here.

Dad was a member of the local Brethen church where we attended each Sunday. I don't remember ever seeing him take part in any of the services but can recall a time when all the men of the church, including me and dad, went out into the street after a service and we all stood in a circle and some of them shouted up at the tenements about their need of God. Dad didn't say anything though.

One time(I must have been about four) some folk from a Scottish mission came in a big van which they parked near the shops in Alexandria and let a side flap down. Inside there was a microphone and some loud speakers which a man used to tell the crowd who gathered round something about how God was real and wanted them to know of his love. I was very impressed by this and a few days later thought I would like to have a go. We had an old set of pram wheels which had the pram top taken off and so I placed some planks of wood on it and wheeled it off down our street and then stood on it and started shouting (I don't know what I said) to all our neighbours. I thought I was doing rather well until the estate bully came along again, and started pushing me off down the road at high speed with me screaming my head off in fear for my life. I think that was the end of my outdoor preaching attempts.

Mum on the other hand was very keen to be involved in church but was frustrated to some degree because she wasn't allowed to do anything, it being a Brethren church where women aren't allowed to speak in services. She got round this though by going out on to some of the streets around us on the estate with her flannelgraph board and easel and after gathering a crowd of children round her, would tell them Bible stories, illustrating them on the board. Soon this progressed to having meetings in our home where crowds of them would sit spell bound in our sitting room as she told them more stories, illustrating them with a huge magic lantern projector and pictures on glass plates. I can remember thinking how strange this all was, all these kids, most of whom I didn't know, all in our house and drinking our orange juice.

Before church knew what was happening, she started a Sunday school in church on Sunday afternoons which they had no options but to accept and every Sunday from then on we went to mums classes in church with a group of kids from the estate. It became a very successful Sunday school with day trips in the summer, going on a bus with lots of paper streamers being hung out the windows. Mum also started doing Christmas concerts at church. At first just with the kids that belonged to the church, then as the Sunday School grew, she got more ambitious with bigger productions.

For one of these concerts, (I must have been very young), my dad got me to learn a poem, I clearly remember the first line which was "I'm only a little fellow, as you can plainly see", after reciting this, I promptly forgot the rest, probably because I was a bit shy and nervous and my dad had to say each line thereafter for me to repeat. I can imagine all the folk going home that night with a smile on their faces and saying "ah, poor wee Jimmy, he couldny remember his lines"

Family life

My dad's brother Robert who lived at the back of our street would often come round in the evening and he and my dad would sit and talk for ages. Dad built me a crystal set once, that's a small radio which worked without batteries, it needed a long wire aerial outside and you had to have earphones to listen to it. My uncle Robert was very interested in it but unfortunately every time he came round, their talks together seemed to take prominence over getting it to work and I don't know that I ever had it working in Scotland.

Dad loved gardening and had a greenhouse at the back and a vegetable patch for potatoes and other veg's which he worked very hard on. Probably after the war we needed his produce because rationing continued for some years. We didn't have much money in our early years but he always did his best to give us treats, but as things slowly improved we began going day trips on the many steamers there were in those days, either up the Clyde or on Loch Lomond.

We also went on holidays to St Andrews and Carnoustie in an old ridge tent which dad acquired from somewhere. We used to travel out to St Andrews by coach. They were old rickety things , but it was always really exciting for me and Grace. I can distinctly remember the first time we went on one, after we had started out, I shouted out "mum, have we got the goozunder" which was the name for the potty which most people kept under the beds in those days. My mum said "shush Jimmy" It caused quite a laugh throughout the coach.

Half way we stopped at a coach park for a short while and mum and Gracie got off to go to the toilet, unfortunately the driver had parked in the wrong place and he explained that he would have to move the coach, once this had been done, my dad had to get off to go and find mum and Grace, in the mean time, I started to cry cause I thought we were going to go off without them. All the people on the coach were all saying then "aw, the poor wee lad" and trying to comfort me saying "they wont be long now, the coach willny go without them". Sure enough, my dad soon appeared with them both in tow back to where the coach was now parked and I was very relieved.

Holidays in our old ridge tent were pretty basic, but we

really enjoyed being by the sea, paddling and swimming, playing on the camp site with friends that we easily made while we were there. We slept on canvas camp beds and mum and dad cooked our meals on a primus stove, all very basic but we loved it.

At home, our Saturdays were special. Dad and mum would often take us on the three three or three two bus to Glasgow, either to shop or visit dads brother George and wife Jessie.

The double Decker buses in those days had long bench seats upstairs with the isle down one side which meant that providing there was one seat which was empty we could all sit together. I loved the trip to Glasgow, looking out at the passing countryside and towns. At one point in the journey, I always looked out for a set of model soldiers in one of the gardens, these soldiers were brightly painted, standing on posts, their arms would go round and round in the wind like windmills, I was fascinated by them.

Uncle George and Auntie Jessie lived in an old tenement building. Their flat, as I remember it, had a living room where they also cooked and ate and a curtained off section where their double bed just fitted in, the toilet was on the landing, shared with many of the other residents. I thought our visits to them were wonderful, particularly because I could look out of their window and have a wonderful view of steam trains as they would go puffing by with lots of steam and smoke, on the track just below their tenement. Uncle George had been a communist, so we were often told, but had become a Christian later in life. Their son, who was also called George I think, was in the Boys Brigade and had a bugle which was fascinating to me and I would always look at it on the shelf and want to have a go with it. Of course, it really was a horrible place where they lived, as many people did in Glasgow in those days. It must have been a welcome relief when they occasionally would come to visit us in Alexandria. Their visit would generally culminate in Auntie Jessie taking a turn on our organ, which she played very well and singing hymns with her warbling voice, as she furiously pedalled away on the bellows.

Our return journey from Glasgow sometimes must have been quite late in the evening and possibly because it was dark and I had nothing to look at, I would imagine myself to be the driver and make all the engine noises. I can only think the rest of the bus must have been relieved when I eventually tired of this and went to sleep.

Later in life when I got married, my wife Jean and I went up to visit my relatives in Scotland and was pleased to find that George and Jessie, in their old age now had a lovely modern house, in the suburbs of Glasgow, but amazingly, they still had a railway at the end of their back garden but now they were diesel trains which was better for them.

Day trips

As mentioned before, day trips were very popular in Scotland in those days, especially on the steamers that were either on the Clyde or on Loch Lomond. I loved these trips as a young lad, the paddle steamers especially were so exiting. You could go below decks and watch the oil fired steam engines, the large pistons pushing and pulling the huge crank shaft which drove the paddles each side of the ship. The engineer watching the various dials and pulling levers and occasionally squirting some oil onto moving parts. On each side of the engine room there were observation windows where you could see the paddles splashing away as they powerfully pushed the boat through the water.

.The journey up Loch Lomond to the top took about 4 hours, The Loch being twenty four miles long. In my opinion, it is the most scenic stretch of water in Britain and best viewed from an excursion by boat from bottom to top and back with views of Ben Lomond and other mountains, hill and islands., stopping at various piers on the way, Balmaha, Luss, Tarbet and culminating with Ardlui where there would be a stop of around an hour or so.

I loved watching the man with the rope who, when coming in to a pier would throw the rope ashore to a man waiting to receive it, who would then pull a large heavy rope in to the pier and put it round a big metal bollard to secure the steamer while further day-trippers would embark. I was highly impressed with this and would often practice at home throwing an old washing line over the road. My ambition was that I could be the rope man who did this when I grew up.

In March of 1953, when I was seven, the brand new Maid of the Loch was launched and entered service in May of that year. I'm pretty sure that we sailed on her in that first year. I thought she was the most beautiful steamer that I had ever seen and I just loved her and loved the trip we had on her from Balloch all the way to the top of Loch Lomond, a love affair that has stayed with me all through my life. She would sail up the beautiful Loch amid the stunning scenery of hills and mountains, stopping at all the piers different piers on the way up.

Maid of the Loch as I remember her

Once, we sailed up loch Lomond to Tarbet and then we, along with lots of other folk, got off and walked along the road over to Arrowchar which was at the top of Loch Long, it wass about a mile or so walk. When we finally arrived, there was another steamer waiting there for us which took us all the way back down the loch Long, onto the Clyde and on to Helensburgh where disembarked and caught the trains back home. As we got off the steamer at Helensburgh, I remember looking down and seeing the water through the boards of the pier which made me a bit nervous , so I reached up to hold my dads hand which made me feel better. Imagine my shock though when I looked up to see it wasn't my dad's hand I was holding but some other man, mum and dad a little way ahead and watching in amusement. The man kindly handed me over to my dad with a smile.

The last time we went on the maid was after we had moved to England and had gone back on a short holiday to visit relatives. There didn't seem to be many people on her then and she only went part of the way up the Loch and back again. Sadly, on 31st of August 1981, the company who owned her, the Caledonian MacBrayne, could no longer afford to run her and the Maid was tied up at the pier in Balloch, where she stayed for the next eleven years, slowly rotting away. I often thought of her and wished someone would buy her and start a restoration project to bring her back to life.

Thankfully in recent years, a group of locals bought her and with the help of lots of volunteers have begun the huge and expensive task of restoring her with the view eventually to get her sailing again

The maid as she was for many years

These are our memories of the maid from our childhood days, seeing her whenever we went down to the loch, sailing on her when we could, up the beautiful Loch Lomond, to the accompanied Scottish music, a memory never to be forgotten.

This is how she looks today after a huge labour of love by the volunteers, enabled by donations and grants, a wonderful job of restoration. We still hope one day she will sale again and if we are not too old, we can have one more trip on her.

****
****

Grace's story again

Our primary school, called Levenvale Primary School was about three quarters of a mile away, and together with other kids in our road we would walk there and back four times a day – coming home at lunchtime! I can still remember the section of Argyle Road, (which led to the school) where I would get a bit anxious – someone in this road had a dog which would often be off the lead and it would come and bark at us and chase us down the road!!

Our school was very strict. On my first day there, I remember sitting in our classroom listening to the Headmaster who had come to speak to us. One of the things he said was 'If you don't behave yourself, you will be in hot water!' I was quite frightened to hear that, as I took it to mean that if we were naughty we'd be put in a tank of hot water!!

 Our teachers demanded obedience and quietness, and when I was 6 I remember whispering to my friend next to me, as I hadn't understood what I was told to do. To my horror I was called out to the front of the class and had the strap! (struck on my hand by a leather belt!)   I think that was a bit harsh, but it certainly kept us all attentive and well behaved. I was later to get the strap again from a teacher called Miss Lynch, when I got all my sums wrong!   My mum thought that was too harsh so she came to see the teacher and told her 'Just because your name is Lynch, doesn't mean to say you can lynch the kids!!!!'

In my last year at that school I was very pleased to be 'the teachers pet' - I don't know why – perhaps because I was a quiet and shy girl who behaved! He always spoke kindly to me and I always seemed to have a good report from him. One day, he set us some work to do, and placed a pupil at the front to watch us, in case we spoke or cheated. I must have said something to my neighbour, 'cos my name was called out, along with a few others. He lined us all up with me being at the end of the line, and got his strap out. He gave all the others the strap then bent down and whispered to me 'Go and sit down!' I was very happy in his class!

Broomly Crescent Friends, and Ebenezer Hall

We lived in a road called 'Broomly Crescent' which was a nice road - all prefabs , of course. There were quite a few kids of our ages in the road, so we had lots of playmates to play with in the evenings, weekends and holidays. Jimmy and I played mostly with our friends directly across the road from us – Margaret and Violet. We had lots of fun together playing in our gardens, or in the road with all the other kids, in each others houses, or going for picnics to Loch Lomond.

Loch Lomond

Often in the summer holidays our Mum used to take a crowd of kids to the Bay – the beach at the end of the Loch. We used to paddle in the Loch, or play on the beach whenever it was dry and sunny. Occasionally for a special treat our family used to go on the steamer called 'The Maid of the Loch', which would steam up to the other end of the Loch, where you'd have a few hours at Ardlui to spend walking round the village and having a picnic, before steaming the 25 miles back down again. That was our favourite outing and I loved 'The Maid of the Loch' so much, I decided I was going to work on it when I left school!

The 'Maid of the Loch'

Most evenings we'd be out with the other kids in the street playing games. Occasionally we would get up to mischief, and at the same time we would all knock on the front doors of all nearest prefabs then hide quickly behind fences and watch all the mums or dads open the door to see no one, except all the other parents who had opened their doors also. They would shake their heads at each other and shut their doors again.

Another favourite trick we had when it was the dark winter nights, was to get some black thread and tie it back and forth between the posts of the little alleyways, (which led to the next road), like a huge spider web!   Then we'd hide behind a fence and watch as the adults walking down the alleyway would get all caught up in the thread and had a job to extricate themselves. We would be giggling away behind the fence.

Life was much safer, happier and peaceful in those days – no fears of being kidnapped, or attacked or murdered, etc., and we could even go up to a local stream (we called it 'the burn') where we'd take lemonade and sandwiches and spend hours there having a picnic and paddling in the burn on our own without a watchful parent.

There *was* an area we were a bit careful with, though. Adjacent to the top of our road were some corrugated iron, long huts – I think they were billets for the soldiers during the war. No one had claimed them and they were not being used, so some poor families had found them and had moved in, making them their homes. We didn't really associate with those children, who were a bit shabby and dirty looking. Although they went to our school, they were pointed out as kids from those huts, and sad to say, were treated a little like gypsies. I remember going into one of those huts – I had somehow made friends with a girl who lived in one. It was quite a shock to see how they lived – the floors were very dirty and I was not very comfortable there. My mum checked my hair when I got back in case I had picked up nits!!

A typical billet hut

Church activities and Fun

We were members of our local Brethren Church called Ebenezer Hall, in Alexandria, and on Sundays we would walk to the church (about three quarters of a mile away) for the morning service, walk home for lunch, then walk back for Sunday School, walk home for tea, then back for the evening service. The Brethren Church had quite strict views on Sundays – you were not supposed to do any work, - no washing or housework and no buying anything. Not that we'd have had any opportunity to do any of those – our whole day was more or less taken up with going to and from the church! I enjoyed the Sunday School very much, though found the morning and evening services very boring.

We always looked forward to the annual Sunday School outing which was to a small place called Rhu. We'd go in a hired double-decker bus, filled with streamers. Then we would spend the afternoon playing games, having races and being swung on a long swing hung from a tree. We'd be given a brown paper bag containing a roll, bun, and crisps – which we all loved!!

Another treat would be the annual Easter long ramble our Dad used to do for all the kids in the road – we'd walk across the moors to Cardross – then get the bus back again. We loved that walk, through wild countryside covered in heather and the occasional highland sheep and deer.

Lovely Scenery

From our prefab front window we could see Ben Lomond, the nearest mountain. From the back window we could see the old Tullichewan Castle – an unused castle which lay for many years unnoticed and sadly neglected.

Tullichewan Castle

It was a shock when we heard that the local council couldn't afford to pay the rates on it any more, so they decided to blow up the main section of the castle and just leave the one tower standing!!! Sacrilege – it wouldn't be allowed to happen nowadays! I can still remember that day when we stood in our back garden and watched it being blown up! We felt so sad as we often used to go for walks to the castle and play in the castle grounds which were overgrown but made good places to hide and play in. However, we still had Balloch Castle nearby and occasionally went for walks in those castle gardens which were later turned into a Bear Park!   (not sure you got that right Grace, I think it was on the other side of the bay).

Balloch Castle

There were so many lovely places to visit – I still think it was a great place to grow up. We would sometimes get the bus to Wemyss Bay and take the steamer ship to Millport, or to Rothesay or to Dunoon. Beautiful scenery as we sailed to the Islands.

Sailing to Dunoon

Family Members

My Dad's brother and family lived in the next road to us - Uncle Robert and Auntie Minnie. They had a daughter, Anne, and 2 sons – I can't remember their names, sadly. He also had a sister – Auntie Kate, who we didn't see very often, and I'm sorry to say I have forgotten her children's names also.

The Gorbals (not members of our family!)

Often, though, we would get the bus to Glasgow to visit my Uncle George and Auntie Jessie. They lived in The Gorbals, an infamous slum area where mostly everyone lived in tenement flats. Our uncle and aunt lived in such a tenement. They had only 2 rooms – a living room with a sink and cupboard in one corner (that was the kitchen) a table in the other corner (that was the dining room) and a sofa in the middle, (that was the lounge). Behind a curtained recess was their bed (that was the bedroom). Their daughter used the other room as her bedroom, but when she grew up and moved out, that became 'The Parlour' – the best room for special guests. Their tenement block was on top of the underground train line, and when you looked out of their main room window you could see the ships on the Clyde. So, you would hear the underground trains whooshing under the tenement block, and on foggy days you'd hear the ships foghorns. It was quite a noisy place to live, but Auntie Jessie told me many years later after they had all been moved out to pensioners flats in the suburbs, that she really missed hearing the ships and underground trains.

The tenement flats had no bathroom or toilet. One toilet on every floor was the communal toilet for about 4 families!!!! You may wonder how you'd get on if you needed to go to the toilet in the middle of the night? Well, every family would have a 'goosunder' (A potty that goes under the bed!)

Uncle George and Auntie Jessie loved their little flat and we enjoyed visiting them, they were a lovely, happy couple with a great sense of humour. Auntie Jessie was Uncle George's second wife. Uncle George previously was married to a very dour miserable lady, Auntie Agnes, but she had died. He then met Auntie Jessie and had a very long and happy marriage with this lovely lady.

Occasionally some of our uncles and aunts from Birmingham would come to visit us for a holiday which we loved. I don't know how we slept them all in our little prefab – I think they must have all had to sleep in the one bedroom and all of us in the other – but nobody minded. We'd take them out on the Loch, and visit our favourite places. My Uncle Jack told me many years later that while out one Sunday he bought us an ice cream, and I had gone rushing to my Dad with horror, saying 'Daddy, Uncle Jack has bought us an ice cream on a Sunday!!!' (Even now, I still don't like buying things on Sundays, or doing any washing!)

Holidays

We didn't have much money for holidays – our Dad was at

work as an engineer at the Royal Naval Torpedo factory still – though it wasn't making torpedoes any more.   But he didn't get a huge wage – nobody did in those days! Occasionally a friend who had a little old car would offer to take our tent and all our camping stuff to a camp site in St. Andrews for us, while we would get the bus. We were always very excited to go camping, though our tent was very old and tiny so the 4 of us used to sleep, eat and sit in this tiny tent, hoping it wouldn't rain as it had a few holes in it.

We had some friends who lived in Morecambe, so occasionally they would visit us and we would go to Morecambe for our holiday.

****
****

Jimmy

School days

Somewhere around the age of five I started school at the Vale of Leven Infants/ Junior School. It happened one sunny morning, standing on the front door step, I wondered why I was up so early and dressed in new little shorts and jacket and why the sun was so low in the sky. The school was about a ten minute walk, down our road, over the main road and down Argyll Street. Mum used to walk me down with Grace each morning to start with and collect me at dinner time to go back home for something to eat, back again and collect me at three. One day, not too long after I had started, mum must have had to go off somewhere for the day so she gave me some money to hand in to the teacher for me to stay for a school dinner. I mustn't have understood this properly or maybe forgot, I don't know. Any way, I came out at dinner time as usual to find, rather disturbingly, mum wasn't there. I then walked all the way home by myself, then to find there was no one at home and the doors were locked. Not knowing what to do I sat on down the doorstep and cried. Thankfully, it wasn't long before my dad appeared on his bike, he had come home for his dinner which was all prepared and in the pressure cooker. He kindly shared some of it with me before taking me back to school feeling somewhat comforted.
After a while, I was left to come and go with my friends. There was so little traffic on the roads in those days, it wasn't a problem to cross the main road by ourselves, in fact, me and my mates liked to watch what came along the roads and do some lorry spotting, we would cry "it's a BRS, (British Road Service) or maybe a RNTF (Royal

Navy Torpedo Factory), that was pretty well all that came along on the roads then apart from the red double Decker busses and the occasional car.

I don't remember an awful lot about school, maybe because I wasn't there a lot with various illnesses including a mastoid in my right ear which left me very slightly deaf and I had to go for lots of hearing tests after it all.

I do remember though the times tables we learned, all the way up to 12 x 12 and learning how to write letters in italics having a card with all the letters on it and slots in-between to practice copying them onto paper underneath. Other than that, I remember that when it rained, there would be a small stream running down through the playing field at the back which I like to play in but the teachers didn't seem to be too pleased with this and would come out to tell me to stop it.

One thing I found when starting school, you start making new friends. There were two in particular that stand out in my memory. One of them was a lad of my own age who I quickly got on with and he was soon invited home by my mother for tea. We had a nice time together and when it came for him to go home, he asked if I would like to come and see where he lived. With my mothers agreement we both set off up our road to the top and then turned left to go over the field towards the hill at the back of our house. When we started to climb the bank that led up to the castle I asked "where are we going?".

"I live in the courtyard at the side of the castle in a flat", he replied. I looked up at the darkened archway leading into the courtyard rather nervously and much to his disappointment decided it was a bit too scary for me and it was time for me to go home. Sadly, that was the end of what could have been a happy friendship and also I missed the chance to see what was inside that courtyard which we had walked past so many times.

Interestingly, many year later, when on holiday with my wife in the area, I got talking with a gardener on the site where we were staying and he remembered the castle being demolished just as I did, but he added a bit more to it. According to him, the owner at that time had been given the rates bill which had gone up considerably, he contested it but the council would not lower it, so out of anger, he blew it up. It was a shame, continued the gardener, because shortly afterwards, the planners announced that a new trunk road, the A82 was to be built which was to run right in front of the sight of the former castle and the rates would have had to be reduced had it still be there!!

The stables courtyard, all the remains of the castle.

The other lad who I remember was a bit older than me, his name was James. I
discovered that on wet days, some of the girls, my sister included, used to hang around in the cloakroom which was on the side of the main corridor of the school, and James used to tease them and chase them in and out of the rows of coats which were hanging on the racks. I thought this was a pretty good game so I joined in and quite enjoyed it. As a result of getting to know him a bit I got invited to his birthday party. I discovered he lived in a very nice house on a farm some way up the road towards Luss. I felt very privileged to be invited to his party. In reality, it was more likely that he had a bit of a crush on Grace and maybe

thought it would make a good impression on her if he asked me along to his party. What ever the reason, I was really pleased to be there, the food was great and he had some wonderful presents which I enjoyed having a little play with and which for sure I could never hope to have myself.

Visits to England

While we were growing up in Scotland my mums family in England were growing too. My mums sisters and brother had married a little while before she did and were producing offspring, our English cousins. Jack married to Hilda, had David and Janet, Lottie, married to John had Mary, Joyce, and Deidre (De), Mary, married to Sid, had Geoff and the twins, Judith and Jillian and Auntie Dolly, married to Arthur had Jean and Dean (also De). Jack and Hilda had another daughter later in life, Mandy, who sadly and regretfully complains that she missed all the fun that we all had in our early years.

At some point in our early years, we started travelling down in the summers to visit them all. Mum and dad would take us on the overnight 'Northern Roadways' coach which was probably the most economic way to travel and because it was before the age of motorways, would take all night, leaving Glasgow in the evening and arriving around eight or nine o'clock in the morning in Birmingham. The coaches were very modern for those days, even having an on board toilet. There seems to be very little recorded in history about the firm who pioneered this service in the 50s. This is the nearest I can find of a photo of a coach.

Model of a Northern Roadways coach

It was lovely to settle down with a blanket (which was supplied on the coach) and watch the stars from the windows as we travelled down through the countryside before we would finally drop off to sleep, waking up in the morning to find ourselves in England, still travelling towards our destination of Birmingham.

We were privileged to be able to stay with uncle Arthur and auntie Dolly who had a farm in Hopwood, Worcestershire, just south of the city of Birmingham. In those days, before mechanisation, farming was very labour intensive, so every summer, all the family would join them to help with the haymaking. This was also an opportunity for us see them all and especially good for my mum to spend time with her family. For Grace and me it was a chance to meet up with and play with our English cousins, all ten of them.

Staying on the farm was a wonderfull experience. Although the house was quite a big one, I think it only had three or four bedrooms so I can only imagine that mum and dad, Grace and me all shared one room. It was lovely to wake up on a sunny morning, with the window open and hear the hens clucking and crowing, pigs grunting, cattle lowing

and all the farmyard smells wafting in. I loved it.
The farm consisted of 32 acres, split into six fields, one of them an orchard. The farm yard had barns for hay and storage, pig sty's, sheds to keep hens, a small milking parlour and a dairy where they kept the eggs etc. It was a real adventure playground for us all, clambering up onto the hay stack in the barn, making dens in the sheds and playing on the old tractor.
I was fascinated with the tractor and loved to climb up into the hard metal seat and play with the controls. It was pretty safe, these old tractors had no batteries and had to be cranked by hand by a strong person to get them started, it was no easy job, even for those who new what they were doing.
Haymaking was great fun for us, maybe hard work for the grown ups though. It would start with the tall grass being cut by the mower which was towed round the field by the tractor in ever decreasing circles until all was cut. It was then left to dry for a few days in the sun, but had to be turned to help it dry quicker. This was done by us all going out with pitch forks and shaking and fluffing it up into loose piles to let the air blow through it. Only when it was dry enough was it ready to be collected and put into the barn as food for the winter for the cattle. To gather it in to the barn, everybody would go out on the tractor and trailer down to the hay field and the uncles and aunt's would gather the hay in small piles and toss them up onto the trailer where one of the uncles would stack it methodically, trying to get as much on it in one go and hopefully get it back to the farmyard without it falling off. On the return journey, we would all clamber up on top of the hay on the trailer and enjoy the ride slowly back to the yard where it was unloaded into the barn. These were the days before health and safety regulations, so us kids had a wonderful

time riding on the tractors and trailers, I can't remember any of us coming to any harm fortunately.

Uncle John on the trailer, Granny and Granddad, me and Grace on the tractor

I remember on one occasion, after having spent a tiring day tossing hay with mum and dad and a few others, that on the next day, when it was announced that we were going haymaking again, I thought I would give it a miss as it was hard work for a little fellow like me, so I said I was feeling a bit tired. Granny suggested I could have a little sleep on the front lawn on a camp bed which she could put up for me and she would stay back to look after me. This done, I settled down to have a pleasant quiet morning to myself. I hadn't been there for long and was just dropping off to sleep when I heard the tractor start, and jumping up was just in time to see the trailer being towed out of the yard with everyone on it. "Oh no", I thought, as panic began to set in, "what am I missing, they didn't tell me they were going out on the tractor", and I immediately was on my way running down through the farm yard and chasing after them over the fields, shouting and yelling, "wait for me, I want to come". I think when they saw me eventually and stopped, they must have thought "oh no, what's up with our Jimmy now, what's happened to him".

Besides all the hens and other animals on the farm, uncle Arthur and auntie Dolly had a dog called Trixy and a pet sheep called Bunty. It was called Bunty because whenever it saw you standing around in the yard, it would come up behind you and give you a bunt in the back in a playful way.

So life continued on, like many others at that time after the war, we may not have had much but we did have lots of fun and games, both in Scotland and our trips to England.

****

Gracie' story

Occasionally we would get the overnight bus, called 'Northern Roadways', from Glasgow to Birmingham. It would take 12 hours to get there but we loved every minute of the journey. The stewardesses would bring us a box of sandwiches, fruit and cake for tea, with a cup of tea, then in the morning they'd bring round toast and marmalade for breakfast. It was a great adventure for us and we enjoyed the journey as much as the holiday. I usually stayed awake throughout the night, as I was so excited and didn't want to miss seeing the small towns we went through. (There were no motorways in those days!)
Our Uncle Arthur and Auntie Dolly had a small farm in Hopwood, so we would stay with them on the farm – which was mostly hay fields, a small herd of bullocks, laying hens, and a pet lamb. We'd have lots of fun playing down the farmyard and occasionally all our other Uncles and Aunts and cousins would come over for the day. There would be quite a crowd of us –
Uncle Sid and Auntie Mary with their children – twins Judith and Gillian, and Geoff.
Uncle John and Auntie Lottie, with Mary, Joyce and Deidre.
Uncle Jack and Auntie Hilda – with children Janet and David. Many years later they had another baby - Mandy. Then of course there was Uncle Arthur and Auntie Dolly who owned Grange Farm, with their 2 children Jean and Deanna, and us 4. We'd have a great time together, and sometimes helped with the haymaking.

Jimmy and I with some of our cousins.

We always looked forward to our holidays in Hopwood on the farm. My Uncle had a farm labourer called Melvin who loved to play jokes on me. On one occasion he asked me if I would like to go with him to bring the bullocks in for their tea. I agreed to go and we walked across to the middle of the field. He called or whistled for the bullocks, and they started galloping across the field towards us. Melvin suddenly took to his heels and rushed to the closed gate which he jumped over, then stood laughing at me standing there looking terrified as all the bullocks stampeded towards me!! I then made a mad dash for the fence too!!! I didn't go with him again!

On another occasion when all our Uncles and Aunts were with us and we were walking across the field to go haymaking, our cousin Jean and Dee's pet lamb – Poppet – suddenly started running towards me. I was a bit scared of this lamb (which wasn't really a lamb by then) because it was used to being teased by my cousins, who would offer him a biscuit, then when he came to get it they would run away, so he would chase them and bunt them with his horns, being annoyed at being teased! I had had experience of being bunted, and it was a bit painful, so I had kept my distance from him after that. So on this day when I could see Poppet start to run towards me I took to my heels and ran, shouting for help. Everyone stood and laughed at the sight of me being chased by the lamb - who was being chased by my Mum armed with a pitchfork!!

Mum & Jimmy with Poppet at Grange Farm

On another visit from our whole family, all the cousins – 13 of us – decided to play hide and seek in the farmyard. All of us scattered to hide and I chose an empty hen hut. No one found me for ages, and after a while I started to feel something itching!!! I was being covered in hen fleas crawling all over me!!!! I rushed up to the house and was unceremoniously dumped in the bath, then had to have my long hair combed and combed to get them all out of my hair!! Stupid place to hide!!!

Growing up

Back in Scotland again, our Mum became ill, and was diagnosed with pneumonia and pleurisy. She had to be admitted to the Cottage Hospital as she had become very ill and was in danger of developing TB, so she was in isolation for 7 weeks. Our poor Dad had to do his full time job, and come home at lunch time to give us our dinner, then go back to work and somehow keep up with the washing, shopping, cooking etc., for the 7 weeks.

I can still remember the day that he made us a lovely stew which he cooked in the pressure cooker, putting a plum pie in the top trivet to cook at the same time. The stew was plum flavoured!! But we ate it, knowing he was doing his best.

Our Dad was a quiet man, who didn't share his feelings easily. But we loved him to bits and would jump all over him when he returned from work every night. He would be the one who would shout for us to come in at night when we were out running riot with our friends in the street.

Mum was kept quite busy and earned a small amount from doing dressmaking. Each year she would make me a pretty dress for Christmas and the church social evening. I can still remember the lovely white taffeta dress, with white netting over the skirt and little red bows, which I loved.

Christmas was not an easy time for parents in those days. No one had lots of money, so we would not expect lots of big presents. Our English family would send us presents also, which was nice of them. I can remember being very excited when we found we had scooters for our Christmas presents one year and we were up and down our road on our scooters every day after that for a long time.

Our noisy bikes

Another year I had begged for a bike, but they were very expensive, so our Dad had managed to buy me a small second hand bike with solid tyres. I was thrilled with it and soon was trundling around everywhere on this bike – the solid tyres soon wore out, though! Then the bike would make a very loud noise, as the rims of the wheels were on the ground! They later managed to get me a proper bike with inflatable tyres for 10 shillings, (50p). I was over the moon with this bike and loved riding all over our little town getting bits of shopping in for Mum.

Winter was always cold and snowy up there on the edge of the Highlands, but we loved the snow – we had a great sledge which we used to drag up the road to a sloping field we all called 'the half miler', and would spend hours sledging and having fun there.

All too soon I was 12 and left the Primary School to go to

the nearest secondary school – Vale of Leven Academy, about three quarters of a mile away from our house. I was very nervous to go to senior school as my cousin Anne, who lived in the next road to us, used to tell me scary stories of explosions etc in the Science Class!

Vale of Leven Academy

For some reason, no one from my primary school was in my class at this school, so I was very shy at first, not knowing anyone. On the first day we were asked to get into pairs as we queued up outside to march into the hall at the start of the day. I was paired with a girl called Rita, and we marched through the hall and up the stairs to our first class – to the tune of 'The Dam Busters'.
I wish I had been a bit more outgoing, as my 'friendship' with Rita was a bit fraught and she used to bully me a little. One of the first mornings, while we were marching round the hall, she suggested we swap satchels to carry. I agreed, and gave her my satchel and she passed hers to me. When we arrived at the classroom and sat down, I gave her satchel to her and waited for mine. She grinned at me and said '

Oh, I dropped it behind a radiator in the hall!' I was horrified, as I knew it would get me into trouble. I then had to ask the teacher if I could go and collect my satchel which was out in the hall. He wasn't very pleased with me, of course.

Poor Jimmy was having problems breathing around this time – and was diagnosed with having polyps in his nostrils. Mum had to take him to Glasgow where he had an appointment to have the polyps cut out. I can still remember how horrified I was when they got home from Glasgow – a 20 mile bus journey – with poor Jimmy's nose bleeding profusely. They didn't believe in giving you anaesthetics in those days – just a quick spray of a local anaesthetic, which didn't kill the pain completely when they were being cut out!!! Jimmy must have been in such pain, then had this nightmare journey of a long bus ride home – with his poor nose bleeding so much!!!

Dentists were much feared in those days – I can still remember going to have teeth filled, -without any painkilling injection beforehand! When the drill hit a nerve, I almost shot out of the chair. I think they must have had to hold people down while they drilled in those days! I was terrified of dentists after having a couple of fillings, and from then on I managed to cover up my decaying teeth with my tongue, to avoid going to the dentist again. I couldn't even walk past a dentist after that, without shuddering. However, for my first job at age 15, the Doctor doing the required medical examination checked my teeth, and immediately sent me to the Dentist! That dentist was so horrified, he called in another dentist as he said he had never seen so many bad teeth! He was amazed I hadn't had toothache. I was terrified at my first appointment, but was amazed and so relieved when given the injection, then never having any pain whatsoever for all the fillings I had to have.

Entertainment was not very hi tech in those days, TV was only just invented so only well off people could buy one, and it would have probably been a 15 inch screen and in black and white. One family in our road had bought one, so when our little gang of kids heard about this, we'd go into their front garden and peer in their window to try and see what it was like! Poor family!!

Old fashioned Television – only 2 Channels (BBC and ITV)

There were very few families with phones in their homes, most used the phone boxes on some corners.

In the long dark nights of winter our entertainment was either in reading books, listening to the radio or playing our records. I can still remember a children's serial called 'Lost in Space' which we were hooked on, and we loved to dance round the house to 'Music while you work', then have a good laugh with the comedy programmes such as 'The Goon Show', 'Round the Horn', and Much Smiling in the

Marsh'. We loved the quiz shows too – like '20 Questions' and 'Just a Minute', and the 'soap' daily story called 'Mrs. Dale's Diary'.

We only had 3 records which we would play and play till they wore out and became very scratchy – 'William Tell Overture' was our favourite and Jimmy and I would gallop around the living room on our 'horses'. The others were 'It is no secret' - a Christian song, and I can't remember what the other one was.

We had an old pedal organ, which our Dad used to play and when Uncle George and Auntie Jessie came we'd all gather round the organ and sing our favourite hymns. I started to learn to play the organ, going to music lessons, but my music teacher kept calling me '**Dis-**grace', so I decided not to continue.

****

Jimmy

The leaving of Scotland

When I was in my eighth year, my dad became ill with a pain in his stomach. He was diagnosed with stomach cancer and had to go into hospital in Glasgow for an operation. My mum thought it was as a result of an accident when he ran into the back of a van on his bike, but I think it was more to do with an unhealthy atmosphere he worked in at the torpedo factory. My uncle Robert also worked there and later suffered a similar illness.
He was in hospital for some time and had to have more than half of his stomach removed and then was away for quite a quite a while convalescing. I was so excited when he finally came home and I wanted him to lift me up and hug me but mum said I had to be gentle with him as he was still very weak. I was very sad that he no longer could go on the walks we used to go on and was very limited in what he could do.
On the fifteenth of December, nineteen fifty five, when I was nine years old, I woke up early to find that Grace, who was in her bed next to mine, was crying.
"Daddy's dead" she sobbed.
It was a very sad day for us.
Grace and I had to go to other peoples houses for a while to be looked after. I was taken round to a house one day of one of my cousins that was not far away, who was older than me and had lots of adventure comics which I read all day, he said I could take some home with me as long as he could have them back.
A few days later, on a cold damp grey morning, a black car and a hearst came and I went with my two uncles, George and Robert, and a few men from the church. It was

customary for the women not to go to the cemetery in those day in Scotland.

We were driven up to the cemetery in Alexandria which was high up on a hillside, where they lowered the coffin into a deep hole in the ground. I can distinctly remember holding my uncle Roberts hand very tightly standing on the edge of the grave feeling a little scared that I might fall in and a bit overwhelmed by it all.

In the weeks that followed it was decided that we should leave our home and we should go down to live in England so mum could be back with her family.

Arrangements were made for the move, the Christmas Sunday school concert which mum had been working on so hard had to be cancelled. When the day came we said goodbye to our friends, I shook hands with my two best friends, Ian and Ian and on a cold frosty evening with snow dusting the roads, we set off on the bus to Glasgow to catch the overnight coach to Birmingham and a new life. It was the end of one chapter of our lives and the beginning of a new one. We could not imagine what our future was going to be.

****

Gracie

Dark Days

I was 12 when Dad was taken ill. He went to the Doctor who said he had an ulcer, so started treating it as such. He was treated for an ulcer for a long time, until he got very ill, then he was admitted into the Glasgow Royal Infirmary for an exploratory operation. I can still remember seeing him being wheeled back to the ward on the bed after his operation, and he looked white! Mum didn't tell us what the diagnosis was – I suppose she was trying to shield us in our young age. But he'd been told he had stomach cancer and it was inoperable by then. So they sent him home to die.

We didn't know all this, all we knew was that he was then bedridden and couldn't go to work. Our poor Mum did her best to keep life going as normal as possible for us, but for quite a while I think we assumed that he would eventually get better.

I did eventually notice that he was getting thinner and thinner and couldn't eat much. The Doctor started to visit regularly, probably to administer morphine to kill his pain. Mum had moved his bed into the living room, so that we could all be together in the evenings and he wasn't left on his own in the bedroom. I remember one evening sitting by the side of the bed talking to him, and I commented on how thin his arms were – just skin and bone. I think that was when he realised how gravely ill he was, as Mum told me some years later that he's asked her later that evening if he had cancer.

Not long after this – just about 10 days before Christmas,

our Uncle George and Uncle Robert came round to see him and we all sat round the bed in the living room. Jimmy and I were feeling very low and sad – realizing how ill he was at last.

Mum had not had much money but had just managed to buy our Christmas presents – a Dandy Annual for Jimmy and a Beano Annual for me. That was all she was able to buy that year. Jimmy and I had saved our pocket money – one and six each week (1/6p) - and after saving it for a few weeks we had bought a small box of chocolates for Mum and Dad.

She hated to see us sitting there looking very glum, so she brought us our presents and said, 'Here's your presents, you can read them today'. Jimmy turned to me and said, 'Let's give them our present too.' I objected, saying 'Let's wait till Christmas', but Jimmy argued with me, saying 'Well, they've given us their presents!'. So I agreed and later we gave our Dad the small box of chocolates. He was very emotional, knowing it had taken us ages to save up for it, and I will always remember him saying, tearfully ' Thank you! This shows how much you love me!'

That same afternoon one of the elders from our church came to visit Dad too. And after he'd spent time with him, he asked me if I would like to go to a small party he was having at his house for the Sunday School children of my age. I hesitated, but Mum told me to go, saying it would be good for me to get out of the house for a while. So, reluctantly I got dressed and went out. As I got to our garden gate, I stopped and looked back at the house and felt very uneasy about going out – somehow guessing that Dad didn't have much time left. But I realized that I had promised the elder that I would be there, so I went.

I have no recollection of that party, just that when I got home Dad was already fast asleep in the living room.

Mum had been washing blankets, and had had to hang them up in our bedroom to dry, so Jimmy and I were sleeping in her room at the front. She was sleeping on the settee in the living room.

It must have been the early hours of the morning when I awoke to the sound of sobbing coming from outside our house. As I listened, I realised that it was Mum standing on next door's doorstep talking to our neighbour – perhaps asking if they could call the Doctor, I don't know.

I crept out of bed and tiptoed into the living room and looked at our Dad – he had died in his sleep – and it was horrific to see him lying there obviously dead. I rushed back to bed and lay there sobbing uncontrollably until Mum came back into the house and heard me. She rushed into the bedroom and tried to console me, saying 'Shh – don't wake Jimmy up – it's very early!'

Somehow we got through the rest of that night, and in the morning the Doctor was called. Our friends across the road – Margaret and Violet's parents, looked after us that day, while the Doctor, then the funeral director came to lay out the body in a coffin in the bedroom. The custom in Scotland was for the body to be left in an open coffin at the family home for a few days, for the family and friends to come and pay their respects. It was a very weird feeling in our house those few days – but our friends and neighbours were very good to us and helped look after us. Another weird custom in Scotland in those days was that women were not allowed to go to the funeral of their loved ones. Poor Jimmy had to go off (aged 9) to the funeral with our Uncles, on his own. Mum and I were kept company in the living room at home by Aunts and friends wives. I remember just curling up on her lap (aged 13) and crying while the funeral took place. They all came back to our house afterwards for sandwiches and cakes.

Big Changes – leaving Scotland

My recollection of what happened next is rather jumbled. Mum had rung our Granny to tell her that Dad had died. Granny and Granddad lived at the farm with Uncle Arthur and Auntie Dolly. Granny apparently had said to them, 'They'll have to come and live in Birmingham – they can't live up there all on their own.' So it was a short while after that we left Scotland, the beginning of a new life south of the border and new adventures.

From the bonny banks of Loch Lomond to Birmingham

Part two

A new life in England

Preface

It's a regret we both my sister Grace and I have that we know so little of our fathers childhood or indeed his parents, other than where he was born and his mother was Isabel and his father was James, he had two brothers, George who lived with his wife in Glasgow and Robert and his wife Minnie who live in the next street from us and a sister who lived in Bonhill We do know a bit more of our mothers history and family life from the bits she told us as we grew up but still, if we had thought more about it, we could have asked for a lot more detail of what life was like in the early nineteen hundreds and what sort of things she and her other sisters and brother got up to, what schooling was like for them in those days and what her parents did.

We thought, therefore, it would be good for us to write our memories from back in the nineteen forty's that we have of our lives in Scotland where we were born, which we did in our first book 'From the bonny banks of Loch Lomond to Birmingham' for our children and there children's children.

I also thought it would also be of interest to others from a historical viewpoint as to what life was like back then, shortly after the war and when life was much more simple. I can't help but think if we had been able to see a film of what it was going to be like in our present age, we would have thought it was a science fiction film and hard to believe it could possibly happen.

This book now covers the time of our emigration to England when I was nine and Grace was thirteen. We hope you enjoy it and gain some insight to some extent of what life was like before the present age of technology

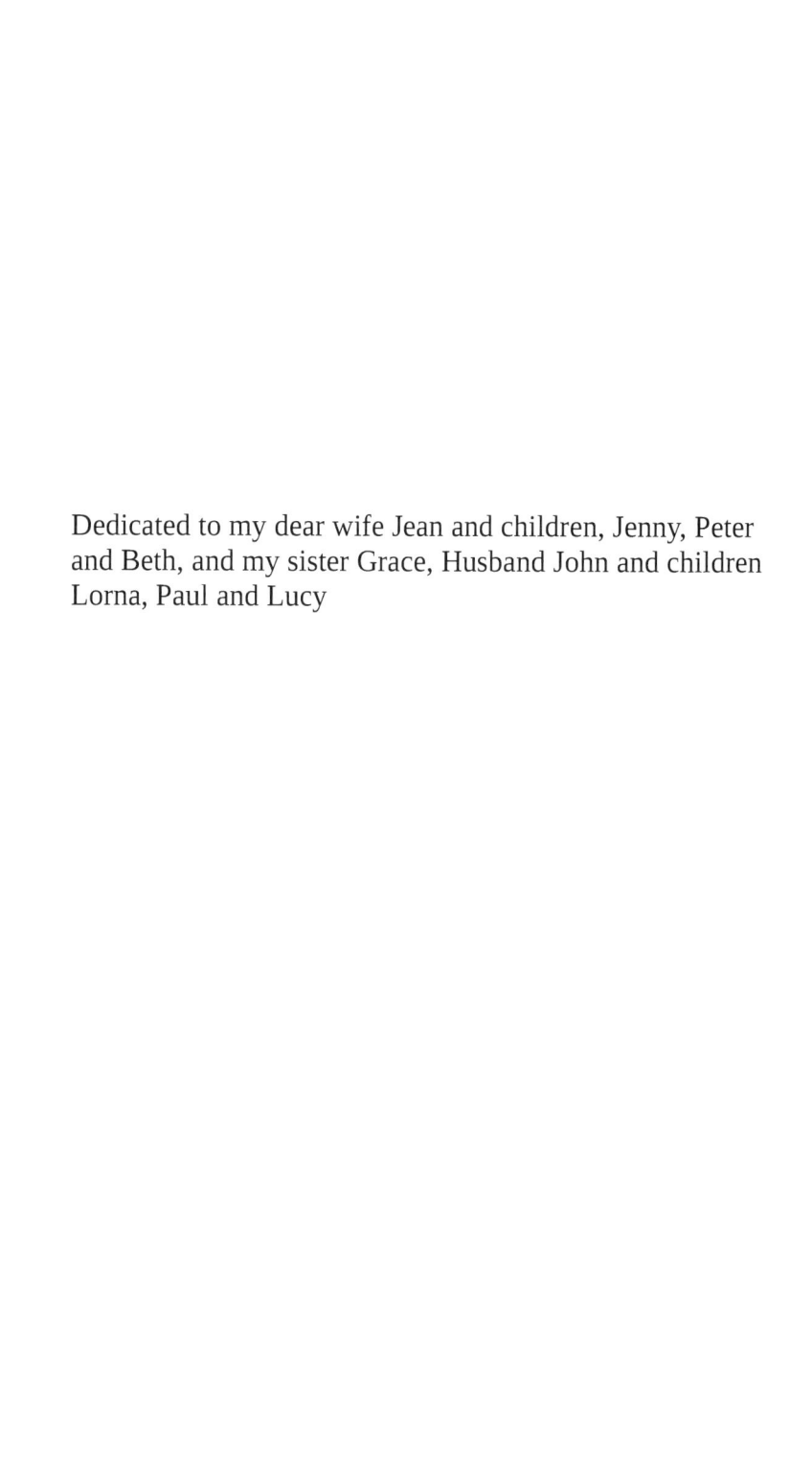

Dedicated to my dear wife Jean and children, Jenny, Peter and Beth, and my sister Grace, Husband John and children Lorna, Paul and Lucy

Foreword of second book

I first met Jim Hamilton and his wife Jean when they came to live in Bryn Goleu, a Fellowship house in Llanfairfechan, North Wales, in 1979.

All I knew about them at that time was that they had been in the Liverpool Devonshire Road Fellowship for a number of years, and had come to look after the house and host the church that met there.

Now, at last, I am learning about some of the amazing things that Jim did before moving to Wales. It is really great to see the Lord's hand moving him along in his early life, speaking to him, giving him work to do, responsibility to shoulder, people to care for…

God does not waste any of our life experiences, whether good or bad in our eyes. We discover as we walk with Him that everything that has happened has been for a purpose – to change us to become more like Jesus, to fit us for new service, to enable us to encourage others along the Way.

I trust you will be encouraged, as I was, by seeing the Lord's work in an ordinary man's life, and challenged to allow God to work in your own life as well.

Sue Lonergan, June 2019

From Loch Lomond to Birmingham
Part two

In our first book, 'From the bonny banks of Loch Lomond to Birmingham' Grace and I told the story of our childhood years, living in Scotland, until the sudden and sad death of our father, at which point, due to the fact that our mother was from Birmingham, we left our homeland for a new life in England. Our story continues from our last day in Scotland, having said our farewells to all our friends, to catch the overnight coach from Glasgow with a few of our belongings in our suitcases, to arrive the following morning in Birmingham. As in our previous book, Grace and I have written our accounts separately without conferring which results in our narratives being different at times, as we remember things differently or even not at all, so on some occasions. We have learned things we knew nothing about in each other's experiences. We have also sought to give some insight into what life was like back in those days when things were so different from the world we find ourselves in today.

Arrival

Our arrival in Birmingham at the end of 1955 was on a cold morning, with old dirty snow melting in small piles on the pavements and in the gutters. Uncle Arthur came to meet us at the coach station in Digbeth in his works van and took us with our luggage to what was to be our new home, a two-hundred-year-old cottage in West Heath, on the border of Birmingham and Worcestershire where granny and granddad were living. (They were our mum's mum and dad). It was only about a mile away from Uncle Arthur's farm. Granny and granddad had previously lived on the farm where they had been helping out for a number of years, but as they were getting older and finding it difficult to cope, uncle Arthur, as I understand it, had bought a row of four cottages, converted the first two into one house and moved them into it. When our dad died, it was decided it would be best for mum to come home to Birmingham and live with them.

I was just nine and Grace was thirteen. I'm not sure we fully understood the implications of such a move, but at the time I think we just accepted it.

My first thought on arrival when I explored the cottage was, "It's got an upstairs!" In my excitement, I started running up and down them until I was soon told by granny that I should stop because the cottages were so old they might tumble down with all the banging and vibration. This had the desired effect on me and thereafter I fearfully tiptoed up and down, much to their relief. I think I was getting on their nerves. Our new home was quaint but also a bit primitive. True, the old toilet at the top of the garden in a brick-built shed was not in use now and a new WC with a pull chain had been fitted in a tiny room created at the top or the stairs. We didn't have a bathroom though; the only place to wash was in the kitchen sink and the hot water came from the kettle that was constantly steaming on the open range fire in the sitting room and the gas cooker. Downstairs, there were two living rooms on the front, small kitchen and pantry at the back and on the other side of the house at the back was a lobby with a backdoor into an outhouse and stairs to the upper floor. Upstairs, there were three bedrooms; the first on the left at the top of the stairs became mine, just big enough for a bed and chest of drawers. Next on the front was mum's which she shared with Grace, and then the other one on the front, which was a bit bigger, was granny and granddad's.

As mentioned, it was pretty old. The windows were small and didn't close very well and we soon discovered that to stay a little warmer in winter in the bedrooms we had to stuff newspaper in the cracks. There were little fire-places in the front bedrooms but I can't remember ever using them, probably they weren't safe to use because we had so much stuff packed into the rooms. The only heat in the house came from the fire in the main living room next to the kitchen. It was here we (all five of us) lived and ate for the time being.

Granny and granddad had high-backed armchairs either side of the fire, where they sat for most of each day. Granddad's main occupation now was playing patience with his cards on a wood board resting on his knees and drinking tea from a china cup. Granny kept busy making frequent pots of tea from the boiling kettle on the fire, peeling veg on her lap for dinner and also drinking tea which she often poured into her saucer to cool before drinking. At first, mum, Grace and I only had dining chairs to sit on and not much to do in the evenings. Maybe we read or listened to the radio, I can't remember. It was not very comfortable though, I can remember that.

The cottage had a large garden, very long with lots of fruit trees. There were plums, damsons, apples and also fruit bushes – blackcurrants, gooseberries, and raspberries – all good for making puddings and jam which most people did back then. Mum was very good at jam making, boiling up the fruit, adding sugar in a big pot and straining it through muslin into lots of jars, then leaving it to set and storing it in the pantry.

At the top of the garden was a large area that had not been cultivated and was covered with tall stinging nettles. It had been, so we were told, a place where previous residents had kept pigs, which fact was borne out by many pigs' jawbones and skulls that I found when I started to explore the area. I had to make paths through the nettles by beating them down with sticks to get around them, a hazardous job, and I was often stung by these horrible plants. I soon found the secret of how to use dock leaves to remove the many stings I suffered. Besides all this, there were trees to climb, races to run around the paths, and it was a wonderful place for hide and seek. Granddad grew a lot of our vegetables in the garden, and also kept chickens in a wire netting enclosure and shed, so we had fresh veg and eggs and every now and then chicken for dinner when a hen grew too old to lay eggs any more.

After a few weeks, a coal lorry arrived from Scotland with some of our few belongings that we had left behind. I don't think there was much and anyway there wasn't room in the cottage for much, but I do remember our canary came in its cage and our old organ which sadly had to be put into an outhouse at the far end of the third cottage, there being no room for it. I think our little bikes and scooters came as well.

It was a big change for us coming from Loch Lomond in Scotland to live in England; there were many differences which took some time to adjust to. We also had to get used to living with granny and granddad and I guess they had to get used to having us live with them as well.

I was quite lonely to begin with and had no friends, so I had to find ways to amuse myself. Grace and I didn't start school straight away because, as we soon discovered, we were just a few yards over the Birmingham border into Worcestershire. This meant we couldn't go to the local school where all the other kids who lived near to us went, and mum had to find a school in Worcestershire and make arrangements for us to start there, which took a few weeks. In the meantime, our canary died and it started to sink in with me that dad had died too, which meant he wasn't coming back ever and made me think to myself and say to God, "Why did they have to die?" It was hard to understand and I felt a bit sad.

I found some consolation though by making a go-kart out of my little scooter. I took the back wheel off the scooter and managed to attach two others I found somewhere to the back of a wooden box, then I fixed the box onto the front part of the scooter so I had a three-wheel go-cart. I had great fun pushing it up our drive and then on the pavement up to the top of our road which was on a bit of a hill. Once there I would sit in my box and, as long as there was no one walking up the footpath, I would set off back down at a fair pace and skid round the corner into our driveway. I kept myself occupied for hours playing this game by myself. Later in life, that little hill on our road came in handy for a few of our first cars which had a tendency to have flat batteries, as I could push the car a little way back up the hill and then jump in as it rolled back down and throw it into gear to start it up.

Finally, it was settled for Grace and me to start at the village school in Alvechurch which was about three miles away from our house. Alvechurch is a lovely little village with lots of old cottages, which you had to go through in those days en route for the town of Redditch. The only way for us to get to our new school was to catch a bus at about half past eight in the morning, which dropped us off at the bottom of School Lane from where we walked up the hill to the small school.

Now I should explain that there were two bus services local to us at that time. The Birmingham Corporation buses only ran to the outskirts of Birmingham; these buses were dark blue and cream and had an open back door.

The other bus service was the Midland Red which as the name suggests were red buses. These were much nicer and had a door on the back, which made them pretty unique and modern for those days. They were considerably more expensive to use though, so if you were going into Birmingham from our home, you would be more likely to choose to walk a bit further to catch a Corporation bus.

While the red buses had the advantage of being more comfortable and warmer in winter because of the back doors, what people liked about the corporation buses was that you could run after a bus when it was pulling away and jump on, or if you were in a hurry to get off you could jump before the bus had fully stopped. "Sounds dangerous," you say, it most certainly would fall foul of health and safety rules today and not be allowed, but I saw it happen regularly without any accidents, and may even have done it myself when I was a bit older! The other thing about the buses of those days was that they all had a conductor. His job was to collect the passengers' fares and ring the bell to alert the driver when people wanted to get off or after everyone had got on and were finding their way to a seat.

One thing about our corporation bus service that came from Birmingham to West Heath (near our home) was that at the boundary of Worcester where it had to do a sharp right turn there was a pub called 'The Man In The Moon'. When the bus reached this point, the bus conductor often shouted out 'the moon'. It brought a few smiles to those who had not travelled this way before. The name of the pub was later changed to 'The Man On The Moon', after the first manned spaceship flight there.

So it was that Grace, aged thirteen and I, aged nine, would have to be up at the bus stop early each morning, having crossed a busy main road to get to it. We travelled to school by ourselves on a red bus and then returned as darkness fell in winter. Nobody got a lift to school in those days. I'm not sure how we afforded the fares each day to Alvechurch, maybe we had a pass or something from the Worcestershire council, but we managed somehow.

Our new school

Starting at our new school in England was quite hard for Grace and me; firstly, there was the difference between our Scottish accents and the Birmingham dialect. I found that the teachers had considerable difficulties understanding me and I had difficulties following what was being said in lessons. On one occasion I was asked to stand and spell 'cinema', I spelt it correctly but was told it was wrong; it was only when some of the class protested that the teacher realized she had misunderstood because of the way I pronounced some of the letters. Also, the methods and syllabus of teaching in Scotland were different from England and I think it took time to adjust. I'm sure it all had an effect on my progress and I didn't do terribly well in junior school.

I can remember some things, though, that I liked in the two years I was there. One was that my cousin Dean was still there when we first arrived. I thought she was a lovely girl and enjoyed occasionally playing games with her at break times. She was a few years older than me, and I loved to hear her speak with her Birmingham accent – it was to me like an American accent is to us today! Of course we also still visited Uncle Arthur's farm sometimes and played with De and Jean, which was good fun. They had a tape recorder (very rare for those days), a huge reel to reel thing in a wooden box. How amazing it was to be able to hear your own voice played back to you! They also had a television in the back lounge in a cabinet with doors. I don't think we went in that room much and I can't remember ever watching it.

The other thing I remember about my time in this school was that once a year the fair would come to Alvechurch. It was only a small one consisting of several stalls where you could throw hoops or ping pong balls to win prizes, and various other stalls. It filled the car park of the Red Lion pub in the village centre. How exciting it was to dash down there after school and look around at it all with the bright coloured lights, seeing people walking around with the prize they had won – mostly a goldfish in a bag. We wouldn't have a lot of time at the fair though before the red bus arrived to take us home.

Home life

Life at home in our little cottage, living with granny and granddad steadily settled into a routine. Whoever was up first in the morning would light the fire in the sitting room so there would be a little warmth in the room for those who got up later. We would have a quick wash in the kitchen sink, have our corn flakes and maybe a slice of bread which we would put on a toasting fork and hold in front of the fire till golden brown, and then after breakfast we'd set off up to the main road for the bus to school.

We didn't have much money to start with, so initially mum started doing dressmaking for people locally. I don't think she did this for long though, as I can remember one lady who was very fussy kept coming back saying she wasn't happy with her dress and she was quite angry, so mum eventually gave this up and got a job in a hospital for a while. I think this was hard for her, it was long hours and very tiring. We often would walk down to the bus stop when we were back from school to meet her off the corporation bus and help carry her shopping that she had picked up from the shops on her way home.

Thankfully, after a while, things got a bit easier for mum. Grace left school as soon as she could and managed to get a job in Birmingham in what was then the GPO as a telephonist. In those days before automation, the telephone exchanges employed a lot of people who would manually connect people making their calls. Also, dad had taken out a life insurance policy which later, after Grace had started work, paid out four hundred pounds. I t doesn't sound very much, but in today's money it would be worth quite a lot.

We were able to buy a few things to make life more comfortable. We rented a TV (black and white of course) and bought ourselves three brand new Raleigh bikes. I think mum thought we could all go for nice rides together in the countryside as she had done in her early married years. She hadn't reckoned on the fact that she was a bit older now, and she soon gave up the idea and sold hers. I think Grace only used hers for a while but I loved my bike and went everywhere on it, and I used it for many years.

After a while, I got to make a few friends in the area. One of them was R P who lived two doors away in the houses behind us. We enjoyed model making and doing electronic things like making simple radios. We put a wire across the neighbours' gardens from our bedroom windows, connecting them to some big black earphones that I had and were able to talk to each other or listen to each other's radio at night when we went to bed.

It was not always the best of friendships for me though. He was a few years older than me and into older boy things. He had a bow that he had made from a branch cut from a tree in the woods over in the local fields and a real arrow bought from a sports shop. This seemed pretty cool to me so I made one as well and with a few of his friends, we would go over the local farmers' fields to see what we could shoot at. It was on one of these walks as we played in a dell shooting arrows at tree stumps that I had one of a few times when my life was amazingly or even divinely preserved.

One of the lads took aim at a tree near to where we were all standing. We all moved away from it but I went in the opposite direction to all the others. Noticing that I was on my own now, I turned back to join them, but that was just as he released the arrow, which came straight for me. I stood there frozen to the spot and watched in slow motion as it sped through the air. Amazingly, it missed my body but pierced the inside of my trouser leg above the knee; another inch or so and it could have hit an artery in my leg. It doesn't bear thinking about!

I didn't tell my mother, of course, I just said I had caught it on some barbed wire while climbing over a fence. She was not pleased.

Things came to a head a few days later with my interest in archery. I decided to do some target practice in our garden with my bow and arrow. I set up a cardboard box in the middle of the garden and went to the top end and took aim. Unfortunately, I made two serious mistakes. Firstly, I should have been aiming away from the house, not towards it. Secondly, I doubted the strength of my homemade bow and as a result, aimed slightly high. My released arrow shot straight towards our sitting room window, behind which my granddad was in his armchair, happily playing his usual game of patience with his back to the window. The arrow hit the bottom of the pane with a terrific bang and sent a crack in the glass from bottom to top.

My immediate thought was to hide, like Adam and Eve when they realized they had done something terribly wrong, but I quickly knew that this would be useless and just stood there terrified waiting for my punishment. A short while later my mum appeared in the doorway. She had been on the receiving end of granddad's wrath, and promised she would pay for the repair and make me get rid of my bow. While I was upset and sorry for what I had done, I think I was more upset that because of my bad aim my days of archery were over. With the help of a saw borrowed from R, I cut my bow in half and gave away my arrow.

My friendship with this set of friends came to an abrupt end shortly after these events. We had gone over the fields in the winter, and on a hillside had found patches of wet snow where we had a snowball fight, and I ended up getting pretty wet. On my return home, I tried to creep in without my mum seeing me, but as the front door of our cottage led straight into the sitting room, there was little chance of that. Mum was horrified at the sight of me and told me straight that I could no longer hang around with this group of lads.

One thing that came out of my friendship with R though was that he introduced me to the Scouts, but that's another story for later.**A new friend**

After that I made friends with another boy of about the same age. C lived in a modern semi-detached house just a few hundred yards away. Once again, like R, he lived within the Birmingham border, so went to a different school. His family was quite well off in comparison with us. Their house had lots of comfortable features like a proper bathroom and a kitchen with nice worktops and cupboards. His father owned a new car which I got to ride in once or twice. They were a really pleasant family and I got on well with them, and I played a lot with C.

In the winter we played football after school in our driveway, in the spring and summer we played tennis in a garage area behind his house and we went exploring over the fields. This time I didn't get into any trouble with any of the stuff we did. We took a keen interest in birds' nests in the breeding season and found it really exciting going bird-nesting. This was finding new nests in the hedgerows and bushes, working out what sort of birds they were by the colour of the eggs and then following progress as the eggs hatched and the chicks grew. We were careful not to stay at a nest for too long though so as not to disturb the parent birds, and we didn't take any of the eggs, although we did hear of some people who would take one egg from a nest to make a collection (something that's illegal now).

After some time, maybe about a year, my friendship with this lad also came to an abrupt end. It happened in early summer. We had a few nests in our garden as usual and I was watching one in particular with interest. It was halfway up a fir tree and very easy to get to.

One Sunday, after we had returned from the morning church service, I went to see how things were going in the nest. On climbing the tree, I was horrified to see all the eggs had gone. While standing there wondering what could have happened, our neighbour (a builder and a very nice man) was doing a bit of gardening at the time and he came to speak to me over the hedge. He told me he had seen C that morning creep into the garden while we were out and climb the tree and take all the eggs. I could not believe it and was very sad but also angry that he could do such a thing as this to us, and next time I saw him I told him that I would not be his friend anymore. So that was that.

Winters

The winter of 1957 was a particularly cold snowy one which went on for quite a while. My friend C and I had lots of fun as over the fields from C's house was a pretty good hill where a lot of children from the area would gather at weekends with sledges of all shapes and sizes. Our sledge was a home-made wooden one which didn't go as fast as some of the others, but it was still good fun. We also had a great time in our garden. C and I built two walls of snow facing each other and would have snowball fights while taking cover from each other's snowballs from behind our wall. We'd keep up our fight until eventually we were too cold to carry on, then we'd have to retreat into our cottage to dry out and warm up in front of the coal fire.

Our bedroom windows during this time were permanently iced up on the inside, and even with newspapers filling the gaps in the window frames, the cold just penetrated. At night you undressed as quickly as possible and snuggled up to a hot water bottle under a mound of blankets that weighed heavy on you, and in the morning you dreaded having to get out of bed. You would dress so quickly and get downstairs to huddle around the fire in the sitting room which mum had lit when she got up earlier.

It seemed to snow nearly every winter back then, maybe only for a short time but it did make life difficult for people. One year I remember, it snowed very heavily in the afternoon and soon all the traffic came to a standstill. The council at that time didn't have salt to put on the roads; instead, they used some black grit stuff which men shovelled off the backs of lorries onto the main roads. It didn't melt the snow, it just gave the cars and buses a little bit more grip. What a dirty mess the roads were in though when the thaw came!

Poor Grace had a terrible time getting back home from work in Birmingham on the bus, a journey which normally took about an hour took all evening. When Grace reached the bus terminus she still had a fifteen-minute walk to our cottage. She was frozen when she got in and had to have a hot bath and get straight to bed.

On another occasion, we had fog or smog as it was then, because of all the coal fires putting smoke into the air. The smog was so thick that night that some of the passengers had to get off the bus and walk in front holding a white piece of cloth or paper to lead the driver in the right direction. Once again Grace had a painfully slow journey home which took hours.

Changes at home

Around this time, there were some changes in the three cottages where we lived. The next-door cottage, number three, was about half the size of ours and had a nice couple living there. The man had a motor scooter which the couple would travel on together. I remember once he gave me a ride on it down to our local shops in West Heath. I found it both exhilarating and scary at the same time, feeling the vibration of the engine and the great speed we went. The wind blew through my hair, we leaned over to one side as we went around the big roundabout at the end of the road – wow, it was great!

Then there was the next cottage, number four: although it was longer than number three, it was also small, it had a lower roof and therefore had lower ceilings inside. A middle-aged couple had lived there since before we arrived. We didn't know them very well, but we often heard them shouting and arguing. One night I remember they had a big fight and the next thing we knew was the husband leaving with a case in his hand, saying he'd had enough. The wife left shortly after that and the end cottage became vacant. Granny and Granddad happily took advantage of the vacated cottage and were soon comfortably settled there.

This of course now made things made thing much easier for us in our cottage. Grace was able to move into Granny and Granddad's room and mum could now have a room to herself. Mum also set to and started to redecorate. I don't think she had ever done any papering before, but undaunted she set out to have a go at it.

Back then there weren't any B&Qs or DIY shops that we take for granted today; we only had the chandler's shop down in West Heath. In this small shop, they sold everything from coal buckets and brooms to small tools, paint and a small selection of wallpaper. Mum found a paper that had a pattern of bamboo and tree branches which she liked. Before she could buy it though, the shop keeper had to run each roll through a machine to trim their sides, as the wallpaper printers for some reason left a quarter of an inch on each side with no pattern on it.

Mum did a pretty good job of the lounge considering the tools she had to do it with. She used her dressmaking scissors to cut the paper and the dining table to paste on. Unfortunately, the only thing she didn't have was a plumb line, so the result was that you could see the pattern sloping downwards from the ceiling all the way around the room. It still looked pretty good though for a first attempt. Encouraged by this, she then set about papering my room, and took me down to the chandlers again to choose a paper. In the small selection there, I found one with colourful little fish on that I liked, so after the mandatory trimming it was bought, and soon mum skilfully had it on my walls in my little bedroom. I hadn't anticipated, however, that going to bed for the next several years was like going into a fish tank!

Next on the list was our other lounge which we didn't really use, other than to go through it to get to the bedrooms upstairs. We bought a coal-effect electric fire which fitted nicely in the more modern fireplace that had been installed before we arrived, then mum bought a couple of new armchairs and a bed-settee. We moved the telly into this room and at last we had a comfortable room to sit in in the evenings.

Life took on a happier routine for us now. I would get in from school around 4.30, have a drink and a snack, then television started at 5.00 with children's hour. I suppose I should really have been getting on with my homework, but Popeye cartoons were too much of a temptation for me, and with other programmes that kept me spellbound, homework stood no chance. At 6.00 pm there was an interval on television. Grace would be back now from work, so we had tea and waited for the picture of a river, which showed during the interval, to end, and the evening programmes would start. I suppose the people at the TV stations had their tea too at this point. After tea came the evening programmes, such as Dixon of Dock Green, Emergency Ward Ten, This is Your Life.

Somewhere around this period the ITV channel also started which gave some alternative programmes to watch, interspersed with adverts. In those early days, TV came to an end at 12.00 o'clock with a five-minute epilogue and then the picture faded to a little dot in the middle, signalling it was bedtime.

Sundays

Mum was still very involved in church, so on Sundays we all went with her to the Baptist church, a very popular one in the area and about a half hour's walk away. Grace made a lot of friends there through the youth club; they had lots of good fun things to do like bathtub races, midnight rambles etc. The church had a very popular minister at the time called Colin Marchant. While he was there, they had to build an extension onto the church to get everybody in who wanted to join.

There were no shops open on a Sunday in those days so after the morning service we would come home, have dinner, listen to records on the gramophone such as Jim Reeves – 'My Cathedral', or Mario Lanza – 'I'll walk with God', and then maybe play out in the garden. After tea, which was usually tinned fruit and condensed milk with bread and butter, a real treat, we would have our half hour walk back to church for the evening service. I have to admit that church at that time didn't do much for me and I was more interested in getting home afterwards to watch Sunday night at the London Palladium.

The Boy Scouts

As mentioned before, my friend R had invited me to join the Scouts in the local unit which met about half a mile away from us. I didn't know much about them, what they did or why, but the uniform looked good and my mum said she would buy me one, so after an interview with a nice scoutmaster, a man in his mid-twenties, also in a smart uniform, I joined up.

The scout motto is '**Be prepared.**' I'm not sure that I **was** prepared for all that was to follow. The Scout group was split into small patrols, maybe three or four of them, called after birds. I was assigned to the Kestrels, another was the Falcons, and I can't remember the others. There were ongoing activities each week to earn points for the patrols in a competition to see who could be the best. In one competition I remember we were split into two groups. In our group, we were all given a balloon and sent off into the dark country lanes with the aim of getting back to the Scout hut with our balloons still safely inflated. The other side was given the task of catching us, bursting our balloons before we could get them safely back to base. Of course, we spent the evening cautiously creeping around and then finding our way back. Unfortunately, we hadn't anticipated the other group's tactics; they had set up a trap so that on our return they jumped out on us and burst the lot.

We also were encouraged to earn badges. I managed to get my knots badge (only just) and maybe one or two others, but I struggled with a lot of these activities. Also, we played team games that involved racing in one form or another. Some of the games I found to be a bit rough and didn't always enjoy them as much as the other lads did. On one occasion we had a boxing tournament. For some reason I was chosen to represent the Kestrels; they advised me just to keep my gloves up and I would be all right. I managed to get through the three rounds but was exhausted at the end of it and was sure the other lad had been better than me. To my surprise, I found I had won, much to the great joy of the rest of my patrol.

Then there were the weekend camping adventures. The first one I went on was just with the lads from the Kestrel patrol, plus the Scout leader of course. We rolled up on the Friday after tea with our sleeping bags and other essentials, packed them along with the tents and provisions into a big cart with large wooden wheels and a long handle on the front, and set off pulling and pushing it for two miles to the farmer's field where it was arranged for us to camp. Once there we set about erecting our tents, one for us lads (about six of us), a food tent and a smaller single tent for the Scout leader. Next, we set up the camp kitchen and made a fire from whatever wood we could find from the nearby trees and hedges, to cook our tea, which we were all ready for by now.

That evening when all the chores were done and it was getting dark, we all sat around a blazing campfire and sang songs and chanted the funny little ditties that Scouts do on these occasions. The only one that sticks in my memory now is this:

> *I put my hand in a woodpecker's hole*
> *and the woodpecker said,*
> *God bless my soul,*
> *take it out,*
> *take it out,*
> *remooove it!*

Maybe it's one that you would prefer not to stick in your memory, I don't know. After this, we had mugs of hot chocolate and for a special treat, the Scoutmaster's wife had made us a lovely fruit loaf. He cut a slice for each one of us which we all thoroughly enjoyed, it was really delicious and it finished the evening off.

I was certainly tired by this point and glad to be able to get my pyjamas on and climb into my sleeping bag, which was laid out on the groundsheet among all the other lads. I had been warned that sometimes they'd play tricks on each other in the night (like putting toothpaste on someone's eyebrows or maybe you would wake up with a moustache), but despite this, as soon as my head was on my pillow, I was asleep. At some point in the middle of the night when all was quiet, except for the hooting of an owl, I woke up feeling rather uncomfortable, as it felt as if I was lying on a load of bottle and cans. As I came round slowly, I realised that I was also now alone in the tent. It was only when I got up to look outside that I realised that somehow I was now in the food tent! How strange, I thought, as I gathered up my sleeping bag, wondering how I got there, and crept back into our tent. My bare feet on the cold dewy grass made me shiver a bit and I was glad to get back in my sleeping bag among the other lads.

I was soon asleep again but woke in the morning to the laughs of the lads who told me that I had gone to sleep so quickly that they had picked me up in my sleeping bag and dumped me in the food tent, and I never woke up or knew anything about it till the middle of the night.

We washed in cold water, had breakfast with mugs of tea from the campfire which we had re-lit, then there was a morning of adventurous games. After we'd had lunch, I was doing the washing up when the scout leader came over to me and said, 'We'll have the rest of the cake tonight.' Unfortunately, I thought he said, 'You can eat the rest of the cake if you like.' It does sound a bit similar, don't you think? Well, later in the afternoon when we were having a break from all our activities, I went up into the food tent and ate most of the remainder of the cake (it was a bit too much for me to manage it all). That evening, after we'd had our tea and done all the washing up, we settled down to campfire songs again, sitting around a roaring campfire, and then our final drink of hot chocolate before bed. At this point, the Scoutmaster let drop that, unfortunately, we couldn't have any more cake as someone had been in and eaten it all. 'Oh but, sir' I said, 'I thought you said ---------

I felt terribly embarrassed at what an awful mistake I'd made as I looked at all the disappointed eyes fixed on me. Maybe they thought I'd done it to get my own back on them or something. Anyway, apart from disappointment, they didn't hold it against me and forgot about it. That's something I've never been able to do, but it is a good tale to tell and laugh about with friends in later life.

I went on one more camp with them before deciding to give up on the Scouts (probably because it was just a bit too adventurous and rough for me). The whole Scout group went on this one. The main thing that stands out in my memory of this camp is that we were all put in our patrols, and given a map and a compass per patrol. We were then given a compass heading which we were told strictly to keep to, only to deviate from it if we came to obstacles we couldn't get through or farmer's fields that had crops or corn which we should go round. If we came to streams or rivers we were supposed to find a way to cross them, even if it meant swimming. We were given food for the day which we were to cook on a fire we'd lit, and the object of the exercise was to see who could get the furthest away and return safely at tea time.

Our patrol, the Kestrels, was given a heading of due west. We set off full of excitement and confidence in our leader striding it out at the front, crossing many fields, keeping to our westerly heading all the time, fortunately not coming across any rivers to be waded through. When we eventually reached the main road, our patrol leader noticed a bus stop nearby which he led us to, and not long after a bus came along. He took us on it saying, 'It would just be nice to go home to visit my mum.' His mum, it turned out, was living in Longbridge, a few miles away and when we arrived, she insisted on cooking us a nice meal of bangers and mash which we readily ate before heading off again on a bus back to the countryside and our march back to camp. We stopped en route and made a half-hearted attempt to cook our dinner that we should have eaten earlier, but soon gave up on that, for even if we had managed it we weren't hungry enough to have eaten it.

When we finally made it back to camp, everyone obviously wanted to know how far each patrol had gone and how we had managed. When we said we'd got as far as Longbridge, it was obvious that we had gone the furthest, but it also invoked a look of suspicion as to how we had managed it. None of us ever cracked on to what our patrol leader had done. I think it did, however, spoil the object of the exercise a bit for me!
I think it was not long after that I felt the scouts were not for me, time to move on.

Grace's memories: Big Changes – leaving Scotland

My recollection of what happened next is rather jumbled. Mum had rung our Granny to tell her that Dad had died. Granny and Granddad lived at the farm with Uncle Arthur and Auntie Dolly. Granny apparently had said to them, "They'll have to come and live in Birmingham – they can't live up there all on their own." She urged my poor Uncle Arthur to buy a house for us to live in!

He must have talked over this idea with his farm labourer, Mel (who later became his son-in-law.) On his way to work one day, Mel noticed a group of four old farm-workers' cottages up for sale in West Heath, so he told Uncle Arthur who very generously bought them, had two of them converted into one and modernised them to have an indoor toilet.

Granny and Granddad then moved to live in this one, and we came down to Birmingham. I seemed to have had the idea that we were just coming down for a short time, then going home. It was a bit of a shock to find that we wouldn't be going 'home', but that our new home was in Birmingham. Granddad and Mum hired a coal lorry and went up to our prefab to collect some of our furniture and empty the house.

However, we were very glad to have a new home, and Granny looked after us till we got back on our feet again. Mum managed to find a job, working in a mental hospital – Monyhall Hospital – caring for the mentally ill. It was a hard job for her – she was in her 50's by then. She often came home covered in bruises, when the people she was caring for became rather violent.

It was very difficult to find a nearby school for Jimmy and me. We had found out that our cottage was just one house outside the border of Birmingham, so we were told we were not able to go to the nearest school as we were in Worcestershire. So we went to Alvechurch Village School, which was our cousin Dee's school, about 3 miles away on a convenient bus route.

Still a very shy and quiet person I struggled to get to know people in my new class. My Scottish accent didn't help! Every time one of my new classmates spoke to me and I had to answer them, they either hadn't got a clue what I had said, or they repeated it back to me – copying my accent. I got very embarrassed and didn't want to speak at all. However, one of the girls in my class took pity on me and took me under her wing. She was a very pretty and vivacious girl – I would say probably the most popular and extrovert girl in the class, who was friends with everyone. I was amazed and very grateful that she befriended me and defended me from all my tormentors who teased me whenever I opened my mouth. Margaret was my best friend throughout my schooldays at Alvechurch, and we are still friends to this day – though we don't get time to meet up very often.

My very broad Scottish accent was a big problem, mainly because there were no other pupils at the school who were not local children. But even going shopping was a big problem. One day the girls from our class had to go to Redditch for our cookery class. My Mum had not been able to get a lemon for me, so I had to go to a shop to buy one. Into the shop trooped about six of us girls together and I asked the shopkeeper, "Can I have a large lemon, please?"

He stared at me for a minute then said, "Pardon?" I said again, as clear as I could, "Can I have a large lemon, please?" He looked confused. "Erm, sorry?" he said. I repeated my request again, going red as a beetroot, and he still stood there saying "Pardon?" Suddenly all the six girls in unison shouted at the top of their voices **"SHE WANTS A LARGE LEMON!"** I was so embarrassed, but the girls giggled all the way to the cookery class.

Another difficult moment was the day when my granny sent me to the local corner shop to get a loaf of bread. Well, in Scotland I was used to going to the local shop for bread and I would ask for a sliced pan loaf (here in England they're called tin loaves). So I waited in the queue and the owner, a middle-aged Englishman, served me. I said, "A sliced pan please," which was what I'd normally say in Scotland. He said, "A slice of ham?" "No, a sliced pan!" I said. He was looking bemused. "A slice of spam?" he said. "NO," I shouted, "A SLICED PAN!"

He was getting embarrassed now and people behind me in the queue were beginning to giggle. He eventually said, "Erm, I'm not sure what it is you want." I lost it then, and shouted "OHHH, A LOAF!" He looked relieved and gave me a loaf and I shot off home to ask my granny why he didn't understand me!

I suppose those are the main reasons I lost my Scottish accent – in those days not many Scots were in England, so we were laughed at and teased lots, and in the end, I started to talk like they did!

The school was only a village school really – we had the same teacher for most subjects, apart from Art. Our teacher was a middle-aged lady called Mrs Mountford. She would bring her dog with her to school, a large husky. He would sleep most of the day, but if she left the room, he would stand guard on us and if anyone played up, he would bark furiously, and she would come rushing back to shout at us.

Soon I was 15 and the careers teacher came to talk to us all.

Margaret had been working on Saturdays in a bicycle shop, and the owners were so impressed with her enthusiasm, they asked her to go and work full-time for them when she left school. So she was excited and happy about her coming job. I hadn't got a clue what I wanted to do. The school didn't seem to do 'O' levels or 'A' levels, so I had no qualifications. Talking to my cousin Dee (who is 6 months older than me) one day I asked her what she was going to do. She said she was going to work for the GPO as a telephone operator. I immediately thought, 'Yes –that's what I'll do too.' So when the careers teacher came again, she sent for me and asked me if I'd had any ideas. I told her, "Yes, I'd like to be a telephone operator with the GPO."

Sadly Dee didn't get that job in the end as she wasn't tall enough, but me being the minimum height required – 5ft 2 inches – I was invited to go for an interview. I was very pleased to get the job and found myself out in the working world when just 15.

By the time Jimmy left the Juniors at Alvechurch Village school, a new secondary school had opened in Wythall called 'Woodrush' where he was able to go to – which strangely was the school our youngest daughter Lucy went to many years later.

By this time Granny and Granddad had moved out of the cottage we'd shared with them and had moved into their own little cottage, part of the group of cottages Uncle Arthur had bought. So Jimmy and I were able to have our own rooms. The cottage was a lifesaver for us, and we'll be forever grateful to our Uncle Arthur and Auntie Dolly for looking after us and giving us a very cheap place to rent from them.

It was a typical farm worker's cottage with the toilet at the end of a long garden – but Uncle Arthur had installed an indoor toilet for us. There was no room for a bathroom, though, so we had a tin bath hanging in the pantry which we'd get down once a week to fill with hot water from the geyser in the kitchen. As there was nowhere else to put the tin bath, we'd have to bathe in the living room. This meant that everyone else had to go and sit in the other lounge, while that person was having their bath, and no one could use the kitchen until they had had it.

I can remember one evening being in on my own, so I decided to have a long leisurely bath. It was a bit tricky as our front door opened directly into the living room. Unfortunately, I didn't check to make sure that the latch on the front door was on, and just as I was enjoying soaking in my bath, the front door started to open and my cousin's husband started to appear! I shot out of the bath and dashed into the kitchen, poking my head around the door to see what he wanted!! He had a good laugh, later telling me not to worry, he had just seen a flash of pink as I shot out of the living room.

The Old Tin Bath – that's not me!

On another occasion, I was on my own in the house and again in the bath feeling a bit nervous, as I'd just watched a rather creepy film on the TV. Suddenly the money ran out in our electric meter and the house was plunged into darkness! I was really scared this time – partly as the house seemed creepy after that film I'd watched, and partly 'cos I didn't know if I had a shilling to put into the meter and didn't have any candles or torches available. I also realised people could walk in at any time, to find me plodding around the house looking for a shilling – naked!! I'm glad to say that I found one without being caught!

A Career in the Telephone Exchange

I finished my training as a GPO telephonist and was sent to work in Birmingham city centre, at the Midland Telephone Exchange. It was a small switchroom, holding about 100 girls, with the Hill Street switchroom on the floor below, and the engineers' department on the ground floor. I soon got to know some of the girls and made friends. It was a very strict regime in the Telephone Exchange. We had a rota telling us the dates and times of our duty hours – which were very precise – 8.00am till 4.48pm, or 9.12am till 6.00pm, or perhaps 8.00am till 4.15pm, with a Saturday morning duty on those times. Morning and afternoon breaks were 12 minutes, and you were allowed 4 minutes if you needed to go to the toilet while on duty. The Supervisor in charge of our section would patrol up and down behind us, mainly to make sure we were working and not talking, and be there to help out if we had a problem. Some of the Supervisors were very nice but others were 'dragons'!

After about 2 years the Exchange was closed down, and we were all sent to Telephone House in Newhall Street. This was a bit further for me to travel, and as I was not a good early morning riser I was not pleased. It meant that if I was on duty at 8.00am, I had to go out of the house at 6.55am at the latest. I had a 10-minute walk to the bus stop, a 40-minute bus ride, then a 10-minute walk across town. This gave me only 5 minutes to get the lift to the 4th floor, dash to the locker room to take my coat off, change my shoes, grab my headset and dash to the switch room to clock on. It was a terrible rush, but I made it most of the time.

Telephone House was the biggest switchroom in Europe, where about 600 girls worked in the very long room, which contained the ordinary switchboards, Enquiry switchboards, and the Emergency 999 positions.

It was quite a varied job. If it had just been working on the switchboards all the time, it would have gotten very boring, but whenever something was advertised on the notice boards, I would put my name down to volunteer and amazingly I was usually one of those chosen to do it.

I was sent to Redditch Exchange at times, where there were only about 12 operators, which I enjoyed. I went to Nuneaton Exchange for a couple of weeks on another occasion and was chosen to demonstrate the new 'Vision Phone' at the Ideal Home Exhibition at Bingley Hall another time.

I also got to go to the big Lewis's department store in Birmingham city centre when there was an exhibition of the 999 Emergency Services. I really enjoyed demonstrating what happens when one dials 999, and lots of customers came to pretend they had an emergency and dialled 999 on the pretend phone. There were Firemen, Policemen and Ambulance officers there also demonstrating what happened from their end too – they played me up terribly!

However, my favourite job was as a Clerical Officer, which meant I was off the switchboard sitting at a desk working on paperwork, or ringing the engineers to tell them to cut off those customers who hadn't paid their bills!

By this time I had been with the GPO for some years, and was told I was going to be promoted to 'Acting Supervisor'. This meant that when the Supervisors were on holiday or sick, I had to take their place. It was a very boring job – all I had to do was stand behind my group of 12 girls, walk up and down behind them, assist them if they had any difficulties and tell them off if they were late back from breaks, or were talking instead of working. I hated it and could see that I was under supervision myself by the Chief Supervisor and her Class 1 staff – who were watching me to see if I was doing the job properly. I started to feel very bored with the job then, hoping I wouldn't be called out to fill in for Supervisors on holiday or on sick leave. However, I couldn't pluck up the courage to look for another job, so I carried on, just hoping that I wouldn't be called on too often.

Youth Club fun

My mum was concerned that I was not going out much after coming home from work when I was just 16. After having a banana and jam sandwich I would just sit in the house each night watching TV. I had stopped going to church also, so one Sunday she told me that we were going to go to the nearest Baptist Church, in the hopes that there'd be lots of young people there that I could make friends with.

It was a good church with a young minister who had a heart to work with young people. After the two Sunday services, he would finish off his busy day by inviting all the young people to his house for coffee and cake and a discussion. I went along but as usual, was very shy – so he asked a very nice girl called Margaret to take me to the youth club and help me get to know the other young people. She did this very well and I soon got to know lots of great young people at the youth club, and really enjoyed going each Thursday. We'd have games like table tennis or darts, then some jiving to Rock and Roll records, or occasionally our own youth club band called 'The Bluetones', coffee and biscuits then an epilogue. We had lots of youth club activities like rambles, joint dances, parties and even fundraising events such as a bath race (with me in the bath) and a bed race down the Pershore Road (with me in the bed!) – perhaps I was the lightest person, I don't know. Eventually, I was even made Secretary of the Youth Club. I must have come out of my shell a lot by then, as I enjoyed being the Secretary and even gave out the notices at the end.

The Bath Race

My best friend at the youth club was a lovely girl called Norma. She was a very pretty girl, with lovely auburn curly hair, and was very witty and sparkly. We had lots of giggly chats together and occasionally went to town together to spend our money on Saturdays. Eventually, Norma met a very nice young man called Mike, and soon married and left Birmingham, which left me without a close girlfriend from then on.

Norma and I

By this time I had joined the church choir, and was a Sunday School teacher too, so from being in every night I was now out almost every night!

We were all very upset when the young minister announced that he had been called to go to another church, so he was leaving. The church then had to invite other ministers looking for a new church to come and preach. The first one who came was in his 60s and very old fashioned. His sermon was very boring, so all us young people didn't want him. However, all the older people agreed he should be invited to come and be our new minister. For me, the church then lost all challenge and became a very boring place. This old and boring minister eventually retired but sadly the older church members voted in another older man, who was even worse – his sermons were even more boring and not at all evangelical.

I continued to enjoy going to the Youth Club, singing in the choir and teaching in the Sunday School. I usually had about six 12- or13-year-old boys (don't know why I had no girls), and I can remember how amused all the teachers were when one Sunday about 13 boys turned up!

I had a few boyfriends from the Youth Club – I'm glad to say they were all very nice Christian lads who in those days respected the girls and treated them well, opening doors for them etc., but I didn't seem to meet the 'right one' somehow. With our church having such a nominal, non-evangelical minister who had no interest in challenging the church or encouraging the young people, I started drifting and feeling unhappy in the church. A couple of the lads at church mentioned to me that they felt that there was more to being a Christian than what we were experiencing, and I agreed.

I was now in my twenties and had been invited to go out with a GPO engineer. He was a very nice person, and we had fun going bowling, to the cinema, etc, but I was uneasy as he was not a Christian. I had taken him to a special meeting at the church to hear a very good speaker give the gospel, but he was bored and uninterested.

A big change in my life

Not long after this, my Mum asked me to go with her to a Christian Holiday Camp in Scarborough, and I agreed to go. Each evening there would be a meeting with a strong evangelical message. evening, after the preacher had given his message (which had not really challenged me) we stood up to sing the final hymn:

> My heart is fixed, Eternal God,
> Fixed on Thee, fixed on Thee,
> And my immortal choice is made:
> Christ for me.
> He is my Prophet, Priest and King,
> Who did for me salvation bring;
> And while I've breath I mean to sing
> Christ for me.
>
> In pining sickness, or in health,
> Christ for me, Christ for me,
> In deepest poverty, or wealth,
> Christ for me.
> And in that all-important day,
> When I the summons must obey,
> And pass from this dark world away,
> Christ for me.
>
> Let others boast of heaps of gold,
> Christ for me, Christ for me,
> His riches never can be told,
> Christ for me.
> Your gold will waste and wear away,
> Your honours perish in a day,
> My portion never can decay:
> Christ for me!

It hit me like an arrow direct to my heart and as I sang the words it was like God was calling me in such a powerful way that I knew that I had to respond. When the preacher asked if anyone wanted to commit their whole lives to God, my hand went up and with all my heart I told God that I wanted to serve Him for the rest of my life!

I realised that God had been calling me for some time – I kept hearing the words of that scripture 'Seek ye first the kingdom of God and all things will be added unto you'. To my shame, each time I heard those words from God I said to Him, "I will, Lord, but not just yet – I'm having fun." Now, looking back, I know that I have had much more fun, adventures and been so much happier since that day that I gave myself back to God!!!!

Back to Jimmy's bit
Starting secondary school

In 1958, I was eleven years old and started secondary modern school. There was one not far from us, but it was over the border in Birmingham, so, as with the primary school, I was not allowed to go there. But a new secondary modern had recently opened in Wythall nearly five miles away from us, cross-country in Worcestershire.

And so I, along with other kids on our side of the boundary, moved on from our small village school into a large, new and properly equipped school. Here I was able to make new friends, even though they mostly lived quite a bit further away from our home. However, that didn't matter too much as I had my bike and the roads were much quieter in 1958 than they are today, so I quite happily cycled anything between two and five miles to see them.

On the first day of term, at 8.25 I set out from home on the five-minute walk to the pickup point on the main road, dressed in my new school uniform, grey shorts and black blazer complete with the school badge neatly sewn on my top pocket. The emblem was two dogs walking past a tree.

There were a few other children around my age waiting there when I arrived and at about 8.35 a rather old grey coach turned up and we piled on to find it was already quite full. We travelled onwards down country roads, stopping in various places to pick up several more children and finally reaching our new school in Hollywood (Worcestershire not Beverly Hills).

There were three other coaches already there when we arrived, and we all disembarked and entered by the students' entrance at the far end of the school. We were led down corridors to the main assembly hall where we, the year one group, were seated on the floor cross-legged at the front of the hall. Subsequent years sat on rows of chairs further back. After a short talk from the head, Mr Bingham, we were assigned our classes and I set off rather nervously to find the form classroom for 1b. Once there, we were each given a desk to hold our books, pens and pencils.

I was sat on the front row on the right-hand side, next to a lad called Robin, who I discovered was nicknamed Polly (I never found out why). He became a good friend to me all through my school life. Other friends I made were John, who lived in a small country cottage about two miles from me by road but only one mile away as the crow flies across the fields; Barry, who lived in Alvechurch by the playing fields; and also Duncan who lived about four miles away in a rather large grand house, maybe a stately home or something, where his father worked as a gardener.

Over the next few days, we learned to find our way around our new school. It was so much bigger than our little village school where Grace had finished her education. Here there were rooms for every conceivable subject, plus the playing fields all set out for all possible sports.

We were given a timetable for the different lessons we would have each day. They were often in different parts of the school so it was important to have the correct books with you, as it could make things very difficult if you had forgotten something after getting to the next lesson. It was quite something to see hundreds of young people walking single file downstairs and along corridors when the bell rang for next classes to start. There were prefects from the more senior classes to keep order as we went.

Our form teacher for the first year was Miss Mountford, nicknamed Molly Mountford. She had been our English teacher at the previous school and had moved with us to the new one. She was elderly and must have been near retirement then. She was a nice lady if a little eccentric at times. After that, in subsequent years, we had Mr Williams who we called Paddy as he was from Wales; he taught maths. Then in our final years, we had Mr Johns who was a quiet gentleman and a good teacher. Mr Bingham (Bingo) was a strict headmaster; discipline was good because at that time the cane was still in use – but I can only remember hearing of it being used once or twice in my time there. I do think it was a good deterrent in the right hands.

I have to admit I didn't find my school years easy, as I was not very academic. Maths and English just didn't seem to click with me, whether it was to do with me having lost time in school in my younger days due to illnesses or missing having my father to help and encourage me, or maybe I just didn't apply myself to work hard at the learning process, I don't know. I often found when it came to homework that my mind would go blank. Fractions, decimals, long division – what did it all mean? Algebra? No idea! And mathematical problems really were a problem for me; I just used to stare at them blankly.

I remember once in a maths class the teacher asked if any of us couldn't understand what he had just explained to us. A few of us put our hands up so he went through it again then asked if we understood now, but I was too embarrassed to admit I still didn't get it, so kept quiet. That was the way it went with me. Often when I got my work back from being marked I would find written at the top, 'see me' or 'could do better'! Somehow though I managed to stay in the same class all the way through my secondary school years which was good because I liked the friends I had there.

Our class the next year became 2Y then 3X and 4X. I never found out what that meant; was it that we were in between A and B or were we lower?? I think, though, that most of my class were much cleverer than I was so it couldn't have been that bad.

I did, however, love woodwork and metalwork, and the school had wonderful workshops with lots of great equipment and tools. Chemistry was pretty good too with all the interesting experiments we had to do, and I enjoyed art but wasn't great at it. Also, I enjoyed sport, but again was not very gifted in it; when it came to choosing teams, I was always one of the last to be chosen. The one thing I was good at though in this realm was the high jump, probably because I was a bit lanky. I managed to come first one year for my house, Snowden, which gave me a pretty good feeling.

PE was good fun on the whole, and I quite enjoyed it. I wasn't very good on my balance though, and I remember one time the teacher was trying to get us all to do headstands on the rubber mat. I really didn't have the confidence to do it but the teacher was determined that I could, so he thought he would give me a bit of help. Down on the mat went my head and with the teacher steadying me, I gave a bit of a push and managed to get up there but my legs were flailing all over the place as I tried to keep my balance, and I managed to kick him in the face, which sent him reeling. I think he decided to give me up as a bad job after that.

The best part about school though was the play times. Mostly, we played football with a tennis ball, tig and various other playground games. I can also remember vividly some of the more humorous and good fun times I had. Polly and I shared very similar interests. We both enjoyed model making and electronics. We'd often bring into school our balsawood planes that we'd designed and made ourselves, and fly them in break times. One that I once made was in the shape of a fighter jet and the first time I launched it with its strong rubber band, it shot off at great speed up into the sky and disappeared, only to reappear shortly after from behind us having done a complete loop. Another time, I brought a battery-operated bell I had made to show Polly. I put it into my desk to keep it safe during the day but unfortunately in one of the lessons with Miss Mountford, on opening my desk to get something out, I accidentally touched the contacts together, making the bell do a short ring. Miss Mountford looked up from where she was sitting and commented, 'There you are, if we can hear the phone ringing from the office below then they can hear you when you make a lot of noise.' There were smiles all round and I felt a bit bad about it, so I owned up and told her it was my bell. She gave me one of her disappointed looks but said no more.

On another occasion when we were writing in our exercise books, my fountain pen was not writing properly (back then we were only allowed to use fountain pens, even though ballpoint pens were commonplace). On inspection, I discovered it had a small hair on the nib but instead of picking it off with my fingernails I decided to blow it off. When I looked back at my exercise book after having given it a good blow, I found (initially funny, but then to my horror) there were little blue ink spots everywhere, not only on my book but also on Polly's, all over our desk and on the notice board on the wall that we sat next to. Needless to say, Polly was not amused. I had to do a quick bit of cleaning up as best I could but not much could be done for our books. We both had to carefully cut out the ink-spotted pages and rewrite our work on the next ones. Thankfully, the teacher never noticed.

As I entered my final year of school after the summer holidays, when the school bus came on the first day, we found it was already full with a lot of new kids starting that term, so the teacher on board had to squeeze our group in as best he could. I was made to sit in with two girls from Hopwood who were also in my class, but I didn't particularly know them. A friendship soon began with them as we sat squashed in on the bus each day, even though I was very shy with girls at that time.

During that final year, one of the teachers started a dance class in the lunch hour, and one of the girls I sat with on the bus, Heather, became my dance partner and a good friend. We enjoyed these dances and learned all manner of ballroom and Scottish dancing. I left school as soon as I was fifteen to start work however, and she carried on to do her A levels, and we soon lost touch with each other as we went our separate ways.

One more memory stands out. In my last year, the school decided to build its own swimming pool in the grounds. Up till then, our weekly swimming lessons had involved a coach trip taking us from Wythall to Redditch and back, a journey of several miles, to the nearest baths in Worcestershire. They probably thought that in the long run it would prove more cost-effective and take up less time to have our own pool. To do this, they started a swimming pool fund, and we held a fundraising day in the school one Saturday, with pupils thinking up stalls and attractions to draw people in to contribute to it.

Polly and I and another lad said we would do a model train exhibition. On the chosen day, we all rolled up early morning with our own train sets. A classroom with lots of tables had been allocated to us and here we set to and laid out all the rails we had as best we could, then we spent the rest of the day playing trains, keeping them running, putting them back on the rails when they came off and charging visitors a few shillings to come in. We didn't particularly notice how many folks came in but at the end of the day, it appeared we had done very well and were able to contribute a good amount to the fund. Sadly, I left school and never found out what happened with the pool. One of my nieces though (Grace's youngest daughter) also went to Woodrush (now called a high school) so I asked her if they ever did build it. She replied, and I quote *'I think they did, but it was all filled in when I was there. There was a walled-in grassy area known as 'the swimming pool!'*

In my last months at school, we were being visited by careers advisors. I had no idea what I wanted to do. Grace worked for what was then the GPO and I briefly considered becoming a telephone engineer, but I discovered you had to be good in maths. As I was hopeless at this, I gave up that idea.

For some time before leaving school, I had been helping out a bit on my Uncle Arthur's farm during weekends and holidays. I quite enjoyed it so I asked him if I could come and work for him. He was a bit dubious at first because it was only a small farm and he didn't do a lot on it as he had a factory in Birmingham where he worked through the week. He suggested however that I might like to come along to see what he did in the factory instead.

On a chosen day, early in the morning, I waited for him up on the main road to pick me up in his van and go to the factory, which was in the Aston area. From what I can remember, it was an old industrial part of the city with lots of small businesses there. I'm not sure what they did there, it was manufacturing of all sorts of things. I was taken into a workshop where an elderly gentleman was making metal biscuit tins from large sheets of tin which he cut it into shapes with a large guillotine. He then bent them into shape on a press and soldered it all together with a soldering iron which was kept hot over a gas burner. Although I did like metal work, I found this rather boring, so on the way home with Uncle Arthur, when he asked me what I thought of it I told him it was all right but I would much prefer working on a farm.

A few weeks later after due thought, Uncle Arthur agreed to let me work for him on the farm. I do wonder if it was from the goodness of his heart that he took me on, rather than that he needed anyone to work there for him.

When I next saw the careers advisor and told her of my planned job, she was concerned that I didn't just end up as a farm labourer and arranged for me to attend college on day release, as it was called, with my uncle's consent. This meant that I would be going to a college in Redditch one day a week to learn all about the different aspects of agriculture.

Leaving school

It was customary for students who came to the end of their school years to leave at the end of the spring term before the summer holidays. On their last day, they would have a leaving ceremony before the whole school, where, with lots of clapping and cheering, each one would be presented with a New Testament and a handshake from Mr Bingham, the head. I left school as soon as I could after my fifteenth birthday, which was the end of term before Christmas, so I missed out on all that. Instead, along with a couple of others who also were leaving then, on the last day after we'd had our Christmas party where we did lots of dancing and had nice food, I boarded the school bus for the last time and quietly left school. I don't think I minded too much though, I was just glad to leave and start earning.

The start of my working life

In the first week of January, I arrived on the farm at eight o'clock in the morning to the sound of many pigs squealing for their breakfast as if they had never been fed before. Uncle Arthur was already down getting feed ready, and together we carried buckets of dry meal into the long shed that housed around seventy pigs of various ages in eight different pens. There was a corridor down the middle separating the two rows of pens with a food trough at the front of each, into which we poured our buckets of dry meal. The hungry pigs threw themselves at it, filling their mouths in a frenzy, initially struggling to swallow it until we followed up with buckets of water from a tank in the yard, which turned the meal into a thick porridge gruel. In a very short time it was wholly devoured, and the only sounds then were some contented grunts and slurping. The next time I entered the pig shed, the troughs were all licked clean and the pigs were rooting around their straw bedding, starting to settle for an after breakfast nap.

The next job was the hens which were housed in batteries in the hen house. After feeding them and collecting eggs, it was on to the cattle shed to fill the hay racks and check them over.

At a quarter to nine, Uncle Arthur left me after giving me instructions for the jobs that needed to be done in the day. He went up to the big farmhouse which was situated a short distance away overlooking the farmyard. After a change of clothes he was off to his factory in Birmingham where he worked through the day, returning home at six in the evening.

For me, left alone on the farm, the rest of the morning was taken up with mucking out the pig sties, bringing up bales of straw from the barn and freshening up the bedding in all the pig pens. At 10.30 Auntie Dolly brought a mug of coffee down to me. I'd never had coffee before so it was a new experience which I tried, but didn't really like, so I only drank half of it before taking the mug back up to her. After a while, I started bringing a flask of tea with me for break times and retreating to the warmth of the small dairy where the eggs were kept. I must confess, in cold weather I often found it hard to leave the comfort of this small room to go back out into the elements. At one o'clock, I cycled home for my lunch hour with mum, had a welcome little rest, then the five-minute bike ride back for two o'clock.

Apart from daily chores, there are always lots of jobs in farming that need to be done in all weathers, as I was about to discover: mending fences, trimming hedges, moving animals to different fields or sheds, sweeping the yard and keeping the place tidy – you were always kept busy. I especially liked to drive the tractors, which I had already learned to do when helping on the farm at weekends while still at school. On our farm, we had two Fordson Major tractors. Even then in the early 60s, they were both already pretty ancient. They ran on 'TVO' which stands for 'tractor vaporizing oil', it was a bit like paraffin but a bit more oily.

These tractors had two fuel tanks above the engine, a larger one for the TVO fuel and a small one for petrol which you had to use to start it up. When the engine was hot enough you could change it on to the TVO which vaporized as it went into the engine.

It was a bit of an art though to get them started on a cold morning. There was no battery, so after turning the petrol on with a small tap under the tank, you had to turn the engine with the cranking handle at the front as fast as you could until the petrol eventually got into the engine and hopefully, with a loud roar, it would start.

One of our tractors had a forklift on the front which was hydraulically operated. It was used to move stuff like bales of hay or to dig out the manure piles. Now towards the end of my first week on the farm, I had to go and to do some work down on the fields with this tractor. After getting it started and bringing it out of the barn, I first had to go and fill it up with fuel. Unfortunately, I had forgotten about the forklift which was in the raised position at the front and as I approached the large four hundred gallon fuel tank which was raised up above the height of the tractor on a brick stand, I just touched the top corner of the tank with the fork. To my horror, it knocked the tank off its stand, collapsing the whole structure to the ground. What a start to my first week!

I still cringe at the thought of having to go up to the big house and confess to Uncle Arthur what I had done. Thankfully, he was more concerned about whether the tank was damaged and leaking, but fortunately it wasn't, having come down onto a flat slab of bricks. At a later date when we had used up all the fuel in the tank, we were able to make a new stand for it out of some stout wood concreted into the ground, which was not likely to be knocked down so easily (not that I was ever going to do that again!).

After the day's work was done, about 4ish, it was back to feeding the pigs; they were again starving and complaining loudly. Their evening meal consisted once again of buckets of pig meal from the foodshed but also of pig swill which was made up from out-of-date food and vegetables that I had been boiling up all day in a huge vat. It gave off the most horrible smell, but the pigs absolutely loved it and couldn't get enough.

By 5.30, all was completed, and I could cycle home again, feeling pretty tired, ready to throw off my smelly wellies in our porch, get washed in the kitchen and have tea. This was the beginning of working life for me and I was quite pleased with it.

Initially, I went to work on my precious bicycle which I still had from my younger days, so it only took a few minutes to get to and from work, in the mornings, dinnertime and evenings. That is, until one rainy day, when as I cycled back to work after a nice lunch prepared by my mum, with my head down riding into wind and rain, I didn't see an Austin Minivan that had unreasonably stopped at the roadside while the driver adjusted his wing mirrors. I rode straight into it, ending up on the roof, then sliding off onto the grass verge. The driver was not too pleased with me, but after inspection, the van only had the smallest of dents in the back and said he would not be after me to pay for any repairs. After he drove off, I had to pick up my bike ,which was now too damaged to ride, and carry it the rest of the way to work.

My poor bike which I loved! The front forks bent back and were beyond repair. I cried a little but I think it was more from shock than sorrow at its loss. For a while, I was resigned to having to walk the mile or so between work and home, but fortunately, not for long. I discovered that when I got to the age of sixteen, I could ride a 50cc moped. I soon found a shop which sold them and became the proud owner of an NSU Quickly for £25, paying it off on HP.

Before I could start riding my new bike though, I found I

would need a provisional driving licence and a tax disk. This, as I was about to discover, all proved to be quite a headache. No one that I knew could offer me any advice on how to acquire these items (there were no computers back then, let alone Google!). Just before my birthday, I found where the licensing office was in Birmingham. I had to take a day off work and went with mum coming along too for moral support.

The place when we arrived was absolutely full, mostly of men milling around or queuing to get to a few counters along one side of the room. There was a huge choice of forms in a rack. I had no idea which were the appropriate ones for my needs, but I spotted a man of official status and eventually managed to attract his attention and got him to show me the relevant forms. I had never filled in any forms like these before and it felt like hours before I had them completed, and then I still had to queue to hand them in and get my licence and tax disk. Oh, were we glad to get out of that place and get on a bus for our one hour journey back home.

So, on my sixteenth birthday, I was up early and excitedly off to work on my new mode of transport which could go at the amazing speed of 30mph, wow! On my next birthday, now entitled to ride a bike up to 250cc, I further progressed to an NSU 125cc scooter, again from the same shop, for £35 (on the HP again). I really thought this was brilliant, as I could now get up to speeds of 50mph which cut down journey times and made it possible for me to travel further afield.

College

During my first year in farming, I discovered there was more to it than driving tractors and mucking out pigs. In the autumn I started my college course. Along with several other young men and one girl, we began learning animal husbandry, animal feed, arable farming and farm machinery. It was all pretty intensive, and although I enjoyed the course, once again I struggled to do well, due to me still not being very academic, so when it came to exams I didn't score very well. The main thing for me though was that I was enjoying learning lots about farming.

Uncle Arthur started to build up the farm after I began working there. He acquired thirty-two ewes and a ram to start breeding sheep. Also we started breeding pigs and keeping more hens. Everything I was learning at college was certainly being put to good use and I really enjoyed my job as a farm worker.

During the four years I spent on Uncle Arthur's farm, I got to know a few of the other local farmers too. One of these was from a farm only a short distance away from our cottage and after a while, I was asked if I would like to work for them a couple of days a week. Theirs was a much bigger farm than ours and I was already very familiar with it, having explored and played all over their fields in my younger years when at school.

They needed help mainly with tractor work, disking and harrowing ground in winter ready for sowing crop seeds. Then there was silage making in spring, and haymaking and harvest through the summer. The work involved driving their tractors on the roads as well as the fields, which I enjoyed.

They had three International tractors, two small ones and one big one which they called 'Big Bertha'. Surprisingly, I was allowed to drive this huge powerful machine on the road despite the fact I only had a provisional driving licence to ride a motor bike

The seasons

Winters were probably the hardest time of the year to be working on a farm. Mostly, each day was taken up with looking after the livestock and feeding them. It was harder still when it snowed (we seemed to get a lot of snow in the years I worked there) as it would then be a case of starting up one of the old tractors and taking hay out to the sheep, or if the tractor wouldn't start, carrying a bale of hay on my back out to the field where the sheep were. Other than that, I was occupied with general farm maintenance, trimming hedges, mending fences, mucking out sheds and so on.

Spring, summer and autumn were much more enjoyable, particularly harvest time when haymaking was finished, when I would help on the other farm with harvesting the corn and wheat. These were long days, working from mid-morning to dusk and then often going to the Red Lion in Alvechurch for a drink of cider before getting home for a welcome rest.

The cottage

Uncle Arthur at one point bought an old cottage near Alvechurch, out on a country lane. It was small and badly run down. He was always starting a new project to have a go at and enjoyed being busy. Every Saturday and Sunday, after the feeding routine was finished, we would head out there and spend several hours working on the cottage. I'm not sure how long it took us, but I think it was over a year. When it was nearly finished, I drove out there on our old tractor, which by the way, could only be stopped by pulling on the hand brake.

With the front loader digger, I levelled off the garden and after all the finishing off was completed, Uncle Arthur had it auctioned. I think it went for about £3,500 which sounds very cheap today but wasn't too bad back then. I think he made a fair profit on it but I'm sure he would have liked it to have been a bit more.

Changes in the air

Although I enjoyed farming, increasingly I found I had very little else in my life and I was feeling a little lonely. Outside work, I only had Young Farmers Club one evening a week in the village hall in Alvechurch, and on Sundays I often went to church with my mum for the evening service to keep her company. Other than that, I sometimes went in the evenings over to the other farm where I worked part-time to see my mate Joe who was the farmer's son. He had a workshop and was there most evenings doing repairs on equipment or making things they needed on the farm. Sometimes I would help him, but mostly we just talked about things (he was a good talker).

***

During this time I still went with mum on holiday and one year, probably when I was 16 years old, we went to Old Colwyn, North Wales, to a Christian guest house for a week. I don't think Grace came, as she was probably at work. Unknown to us, there was an evangelist staying there also that week, Pastor Tom Wilson, who was conducting a crusade at the local Pentecostal church each evening, which of course mum wanted to go to. I think I went to most of the meetings, which pleased my mum.

Uncle Tom, as he was affectionately known, was a jovial type of person and we were entertained each mealtime with his funny little stories. One day when we were out on the beach I found a piece of dried seaweed which looked just like a giant spider. I thought it would be a good joke on him to sneak into his room and put it in his bed. Next day at breakfast though, to my surprise he made no comment. However, towards the end of breakfast he said that the housekeeper had been to make his bed in the afternoon and nearly fainted when she saw the look-alike spider under the covers. I felt really bad and apologized, but everyone enjoyed the joke which was on me. That night the spider was in back in my bed!

My mum started corresponding with Pastor Wilson after our holiday and as a result, he invited us to go to a summer camp which he held each year in Scarborough. So it was that the following year we travelled there by steam train, and on arrival, along with about forty others, we were collected by a rather old coach and taken to the camp out in the countryside north of Scarborough. At first sight, worryingly, it appeared to be nothing but a group of small wooden huts and very basic amenities, but despite this, we had quite an enjoyable week. Every afternoon we were given an excursion on the old coach to various places – Whitby, Scarborough, North Yorkshire moors etc. There were quite a few other young people about my age, and they sang and laughed the whole time on these coach trips. I was very impressed with the joy and happiness they expressed which seemed to come from their Christian faith.

Now at this time as a teenager, I would say I believed in God, but had no real idea about the Christian faith. I thought that if I was involved in an accident – and they were fairly common in those days in farming, with many fatalities (I had a few near misses myself) – well, I feared the judgment of God and that I would not go to heaven, where I believed my dad was now. So my holidays in Scarborough (we went a few years on the run) had quite an impact on me and I would return from these times with the resolve that I would try harder to be a good Christian. However, once back home and in work, I was soon back to life as it had been with no more thoughts of what it meant to be a Christian.

Our first car

When I reached the age of 18, Grace and I heard that our cousin Dee on the farm was selling her car. It was an Austin A35 and she wanted £25 for it, which I didn't have, so Grace bought it and I started to have lessons. We had a man who delivered bread for us each day in the baker's van and he kindly offered to take me out in our little car to give me some lessons. After a while I also went for a few professional lessons and quite quickly put in for a test. Having been driving tractors for a few years I was feeling pretty confident. Unfortunately, I made two mistakes.

Firstly, I took the test in our own little car which almost proved too small for the rather large examiner! Then secondly, although I was a confident driver, I hadn't learned the finer points which are so important to pass the test, like looking in the mirror constantly and being in the right gear at the right time. So I failed the first time. Undaunted, a few weeks later I took three lessons with BSM and another test, this time using the school car and to my delight, **I passed!!**

Sadly, it took Grace a little longer to learn to drive and a few more tests than me, but she persisted and did it in the end.

The following summer, I drove mum and Grace back to Scarborough for another holiday where we all had a very enjoyable week and where I made lots of friends, lads and girls of my own age, and came back more determined than ever to discover what this Christian thing that they had was all about.

What Grace was doing

During all this time, Grace was continuing to do well in her job, as I remember. At weekends she would be up early on a Saturday, do the hoovering and tidy up the cottage (we could never find anything for a while afterwards) and then she'd catch the bus to town to shop and come back with bags of clothes having had an enjoyable time.

She was still going to the Baptist church and went to the youth club where she had lots of friends. She often related funny stories of the things they got up to, the bathtub races, concerts, midnight walks etc, so I suppose it was only natural that I chose to start going there again.

There was a nice group of young people of my own age in the church at this time. I was painfully quiet and shy to begin with, but I slowly got to know them and started coming out of myself. I even went out with one of the girls for a while, which was a new experience for me. She worked in a music store and she got my first guitar for me at a discounted price. I quickly set out to learn to play and practised for hours and hours, often sitting on a chair up the garden so as not to disturb our household. I'm not sure what the neighbours must have thought though, as I strummed away, very badly to begin with.

In the Baptist church at the time were Ron and Ann, a young couple – I can't remember if they were engaged by then. They often sang together and he played the guitar. He had a friend called John Miles and related a story of how together they had gone out to Spain on a motor scooter to join up with an organization called 'Operation Mobilization'. He told of how they saw answers to prayer and God doing amazing things while they were out there. I had never heard of things like this before and was amazed that God should answer prayers in such a way.

In the autumn of that year, I went with the Baptist youth group to a youth weekend at a place called Barns Close, a small conference centre in the Worcester countryside. We had games and fun together and a few meetings over the weekend, hearing and discussing the meaning of being a Christian.

On Saturday night we went on a midnight ramble over the fields that surrounded the centre and as we reached the top of a hill, I looked up into a clear amazing starry sky and said in my heart a little prayer: 'God, if you're there, come into my life and do something in me, change me.' I went to bed that night not feeling any different, and fell asleep with the other lads in our dormitory.

Next morning, our last day, we had a service after breakfast which was OK but not particularly memorable. However, at the end of the service, to my surprise, the speaker called for any who wanted to become Christians to come to the front. I had a bit of a struggle over this. It is not a light decision to make, but in the end, to my surprise, I found myself going forward.

I can honestly say that this was a turning point in my life that made such a difference. It was a new beginning, the start of an adventure that fifty years later, as I write this book, still continues today.

I suddenly found a real interest in the Bible and along with other folk my own age from the Baptist church I started going to various home Bible study groups in the evenings that were scattered around the Birmingham area.

New beginnings

Around this time I concluded, for various reasons, that I wanted to come out of farming. The main one was that I could only ever be a farm labourer, as I didn't have any qualifications to get a better job in farming. Also, with my new interests and friends I wanted to have more free time; this was proving difficult to fit with the demands of working on a farm. Therefore in the autumn of 1964, having done four years working for Uncle Arthur, I gave him my notice and agreed to work till Christmas.

Meanwhile, I continued going to the Baptist church, and also heard from Ron of another little meeting on a Friday night in the home of John and Margaret Powers, who lived in Sparkbrook on the other side of Birmingham. Here I found more young people of my age who had a vibrant faith and hunger to know more about Christ. I felt very aware that God was working in my life at this time and He was with me.

An example of this was when one night while I was giving someone a lift home in our little car, a red light came on quickly followed by a knocking noise in the engine. I knew enough about engines to know the big end had gone and the engine was finished, but I managed to get the car back home somehow. The next day I was wondering what I was going to do when Jean's husband Mel, who did a fruit and veg delivery, dropped in and I told him about the car. He said I should get down to the farm right away as cousin

Dee's A30 van had failed the MOT and she had a scrap man coming to get it who was going to give her £13 for it. I started out immediately to walk there, no time to wait for a bus. Just as I started off down the main road, a car stopped on the other side and the driver asked if I wanted a lift. I thought this quite peculiar but gladly accepted and was at the farm in a couple of minutes. I found Dee and had just agreed to buy the van from her for £13 when a knock came at the kitchen door. It was the scrap man who was not too pleased to find it sold to someone else and went off a bit angry. I have always wondered what made that man stop to give me a lift, getting me to the farm in the nick of time – could it have been an angel? But then, can angels drive?

I somehow managed to swap the engines myself and our car was soon back on the road.

Big changes and challenges

Christmas came and (I think much to Uncle Arthur's concern) I still didn't know what I was going to do. Maybe rather naively I believed that God would step in and provide a job for me. During the week following Christmas, I was looking in the Birmingham Post at the job adverts and noticed a firm called 'Flamecut Blanks' who were looking for a new employee, training would be given. What was amazing though was that it was just over the road from Uncle Arthur's farm. I went along straight away, explaining that I had experience in welding and was given the job, starting the following Monday. I had been out of work for only one week!

I got on well immediately with the lads who worked there, who were mostly about my own age. They told me that in the previous summer months they used to have their lunch sitting out on a wall by the roadside and watch out for me shooting down the hill, sticking my hand out to turn right into the drive that led up the farm. This was their signal to get back to work!

This small firm worked in a few sheds, using acetylene cutting machines to cut precision shapes out of huge thick sheets of steel to the requirements of industry. I did all right there for about nine months and enjoyed the work and being with the lads. However, I was made redundant after the company expanded and moved to bigger premises, as they took on other skilled men who were quicker and better than me. Looking back now though, I'm glad I didn't continue in that trade, as I think it was pretty unhealthy with all the fumes from burning your way through steel as we did not wear any masks.

I was then out of work for a short time till mum enquired in a factory just down the road from us that made surgical aids. It turned out that the manager had been connected with our family somewhere in the past, and so they happily gave me a job offering to train me in forge work.

This job was making steel rods for leg braces. It involved putting steel blanks about 4 inches long into a gas oven till they were red hot. Then I had to hold it with tongs under a mechanical hammer which bashed away at it, making it thinner and longer. I had to do this heating up and bashing it again and again till the rod was the right length and the same thickness all the way down. I found it pretty boring doing the same thing every day, and it was hot and noisy work.

I stayed with them for about six months but it became evident that I wasn't really enjoying the job by the fact that I found it really difficult to get there on time most mornings and when the boss gave me a warning about it I gladly offered to give in my notice.

Another job

Once again I saw an advert in the paper, this time for a car cleaner in a busy garage in Birmingham. I went along and was interviewed by the two car salesmen, who suggested that I could do a lot better than having a low paid job of washing cars. However, when I explained my plans and that I only needed it short term, they happily took me on.

I really enjoyed my time working at the garage. It belonged to a group of three or four garages in Birmingham called H.J. Evans cars sales (not to be confused by a rival firm P.J. Evans). The branch I went to work at was on the corner of Bath Row and Bishopsgate St. They sold brand-new cars from the show room, second-hand sports cars on the forecourt and older used cars on a patch at the side. All I had to do was polish the cars in the showroom and keep the outside cars clean and tidy. Every now and then I'd be asked to take a car to one of the other showrooms or a group of the chaps from other showrooms would be taken out to the compounds to bring back brand-new cars. These would have to be taken first to the main workshop to be cleaned up (they had a covering of wax on new cars in those days) before they were distributed round the showrooms. This is the only time in my life that I have driven a brand-new car. I have to confess we were a bit naughty though, once we had all had the keys to our cars we would have a race to see who would be back at the garage first!

I got on very well with the two salesmen at our garage. They were young men, maybe late twenties, well-mannered and polite. They were very good at their job, didn't push the customers at all but still sold lots of cars. They didn't push me too hard either, just warned me that if the boss Mr Evans showed up, I should make sure I was busy doing something.

Mr Evans was pretty rich as far as I could make out. Besides the garages he owned, he also had a farm and drove a flashy big American convertible car. I got the impression though he was not a very happy man; he drank a lot and I heard that the police had been after him sometimes for drink driving, but he had escaped them by driving into one of his garages and getting somebody else to drive for him. He once drove into our garage and got me to go with him to collect a car and bring it back to ours. I liked his car but have to confess I was a bit nervous of him, and was pleased when I could get out. I'm not sure what happened to him in later life.

The garage was also a petrol station. Back in those days there was no such thing as self-service, instead a forecourt attendant served you. Ours had about four girls and a couple of fellows who operated the pumps. We were often very busy with lots of male drivers queueing to get into our garage to fill up. The girls would serve the petrol and one with a money bag would go around collecting the money and giving change. It worked pretty well really.

Petrol back in those days was sold by the gallon and you could buy four gallons (18 litres in today's measurements) for £1.00. It sounds cheap, but considering my wages then were about £9.00 a week, it's probably not a lot of difference from today.

After a while I was asked if I would like to work some extra hours, helping them on the forecourt. I agreed to this as it would mean extra money. It's hard to describe the girls; they were quite young, real Brummies, and had to work hard most of the time. I got on OK with them, and they quickly got to know I was a Christian and seemed to respect me for it. When I first started, because I was the new boy I got the job of going down to the sandwich shop to get lunch for them all, something I had never done before. One of the girls asked for a ham sandwich with piccalilli. Now I'd never heard of piccalilli before but didn't like to say, so I just went to the shop and asked for ham sandwich with Piccadilly. Fortunately, no one seemed to notice my mistake and I gratefully came back with the right lunch for them.

One Friday night I discovered one of the girls, Elsie I think her name was, was getting married the next day, so while I did most of the serving that evening, they all had a great time drinking her good health for the future. By the end of our shift she was so drunk I had to take her home in my car – they all knew she would be safe with me – and I had to help her to her front door, she was so drunk. I sincerely wished her every happiness in her future. I never saw her again.

One warm night I can remember John Miles from our Messengers group came in for petrol and was served by the girls. The Billy Graham Crusade was on at the time in Birmingham and he gave them an invitation to it, much to my pleasure.

Towards the end of my time there, the two salesmen had some sort of disagreement with Mr Evans and he sacked them. I was sorry to see them go, as I'd got on well with them. I wished them all the best as they left. I'm sure they would have done well wherever they went on to.

The garage was now taken over by a salesman from one of the other centres. He was an older man, and I think he might have had an army background. He brought lots of old cars over to our garage and I found it quite difficult to get them all washed every day. He also wanted things done his way and was always looking for ways to correct me, which annoyed me no end. Thankfully I only had two weeks left before I was due to leave and go on OM. I was happy to be handing in my notice, but it didn't please him too much. I left with mixed feelings, glad to get away from the new salesman but sorry to leave the others, to set off on my next adventure into the unknown.

Operation Mobilization

The time had finally come now for me to go on Operation Mobilization. In my small case, I had a few clothes, a blanket and sleeping bag and toiletries. I wasn't sure what I was letting myself in for, but right from the first night, I began to find out. I had never been out of the UK before, and had never slept on the floor before either. That first night, I settled down with a bunch of other fellows on the lounge floor of the house where from we were to be picked up in the morning. (The girls were installed upstairs.) It was quite a shock, and I didn't sleep very well, even on a fairly thick carpet.

We were up at 6.00, then after a quick breakfast, a coach picked us up and took us to Folkestone to catch the ferry to Ostend. After the crossing we waited for around an hour till a convoy of old Ford trucks came to collect us and take us to the headquarters of OM in Zaventem, which is near Brussels. By this time I was quite tired and despite being seated on wooden benches down each side of the back of the truck, I was soon asleep while we drove up through Belgium, arriving late at night at the base.

We were greeted with supper, hot chocolate and for the first time in my life, peanut butter and jam sandwiches (there were lots of Americans there and they seemed to live on the stuff, as I was to find out during my time with OM). We were then shown to our part of the base where we were to sleep, a large hall with plenty of space on the floor for our sleeping bags. There was another room for all the girls. My bed was now cardboard on a brick floor, my blanket and a sleeping bag. It was uncomfortable to say the least, but it's surprising what the human body can adapt to, given time. (I went on OM again the following year and wisely took an airbed!)

The leader and founder of the organisation was a chap called George Verwer, who was from America. I met him next morning after rising early. He was cleaning the men's wash rooms and gave me a warm greeting on entering. We were to hear a lot from him in the coming week, and I found him to be a good speaker, passionate in his belief that people throughout the world should hear the good news of the gospel of Jesus Christ.

I had originally said that I would go on a team travelling to somewhere in France, but I have to admit I had difficulty learning the small amount of French needed to converse with French people – I just couldn't get my mouth to pronounce words in any way other than with an English accent – so when half way through the week there was an appeal for a few more folk to volunteer to join a team going to Italy, I immediately took the opportunity to try the Italian language instead. Much to my relief, I found it much easier!

Also, during this first week, there was a call for all who could drive to take a test to see if they were good enough to drive their vehicles on the continent. When I took my test, I found it just a bit too much to grasp driving on the wrong side of the road. I was a bit relieved, to be honest, as I was still fairly new at driving and found the thought of being responsible for a group of people, driving them around the continent, a bit too much for me.

At the end of an enjoyable intro week, having met with the other members joining the team for Italy and also the team leaders, we were all loaded up onto two old Ford D three-ton vans and set off on our journey down through France and Switzerland.

These old trucks (and also their VW vans), were maintained to a very high standard at the base in Zaventem. They were diesel powered, had no synchromesh on the gears and could do a maximum of forty miles an hour. Each truck had three drivers who now drove us day and night, apart for meal and toilet stops, for the next few days or so till we finally reached our destination. It wasn't much of a view from the back of the truck, but we did manage somehow to have the back doors open most of the time, so we saw where we were coming from. We went over a pass going from Switzerland to Italy which I remember as being a bit scary, driving close to a very deep drop on one side and rocky overhangs on the other. We just had to trust our drivers.

When we finally made our destination, our two trucks split up, one for the fellows and the other for the girls, and we set off to start our mission. We were called blitz teams. Basically, we were to travel all round northern Italy giving out Christian literature or offering books and Bibles for a small donation. Any money received was used to pay for our expenses as we travelled round.

At night we would have to find somewhere to set up our tents, cook a meal, have a rest and maybe sit round the campfire talking and singing before bed. Every weekend we met up with the other team to have a day off to wash our clothes, write letters home, have meals together and relax. Sunday was a time to gather together and have a service in the open air of our camping site and maybe visit any local town or village we were near to.

For the next few weeks we had the pleasure of travelling round northern Italy, seeing some of the most beautiful towns and villages, such as Varese, Como, Bergamo, Milan and Brescia, as well as enjoying the countryside views from the back of the truck. I guess we toured all round on next to nothing financially and saw wonderful places where today you would have to pay hundreds of pounds to do it as a tourist. We also had the excitement of doing something we believed was worthwhile and would bring blessing to others.

I remember standing outside this station in Brescia giving leaflets to passers-by, mostly well received with a Grazie'.

Of all the places we camped, one stands out in my memory. We found a friendly farmer who was happy for us to stay the night on his land. It was a very warm evening, so we decided to sleep in the orchard in the open without the tents, in our sleeping bags under the stars, not that we saw them much, we were usually pretty tired and off to sleep straight away. Before we slept though we had the most splendid view of the distant mountains where there was an electrical storm going on. It was too far away to hear the thunder but the forks of lightning were amazing.

Our time in Italy came to an end and we started off on our long return journey. Our drivers decided it would be interesting to go back via the Great St Bernard Pass. We started up the pass in the evening so we saw very little of the going up; we were only aware of the engine labouring in first gear and wondering if it would overheat. Once at the top we slowly started the descent on the other side and wondered now if the brakes would overheat. It took a long time but a view of a town with all its lights so far below us was magnificent; I think it might have been Chamonix, but

I'm not sure.

Back at the base, we met up with friends again and compared notes on how we had got on and how much suntan we had now. We then travelled on to catch the overnight ferry from Ostend. Once aboard, we rolled out our sleeping bags on deck which strangely felt quite comfortable after some of the hard floors we had spent the night on during our time away, and we slept well till we reached England's green and pleasant land once more, and drove back to Birmingham on a coach.

Now I was home again and back on the jobseekers' market. Not for long though, as Bill, one of my new friends in 'The Messengers', worked in a medical warehouse called Philip Harris Medical Ltd. His job was making ointments and bottled medicines. On enquiring, he found a job for me in the area where they put the orders together each day, prior to them being sent out in their vans to pharmacies and businesses all around Birmingham. The job I was offered was to carefully pack the goods in boxes with straw round them to keep them safe, and then they were passed on to the transport section. The pay wasn't great, and it was pretty mundane work, but I really wanted to go on 'OM' again the next summer, so it suited me fine as a temporary job. After a while, I actually got to like working there, especially as the folk were friendly and the boss that I was under, Mr Rushton, was a really nice man. I worked with an old fellow called Fred. He only had about two front teeth and each day he had difficulty eating his lunch, which he brought in a little brown case. I eventually discovered, by accident, why he used a case for his lunch, for, when rounding a corner of one of the aisles, I witnessed him stuffing a few toilet rolls off the shelf into it. I suppose he thought it was one of the perks of the job.

Some of the others I worked with were two older men who checked the orders before packing and three girls who collected the orders off the shelves and brought them to the checking area. Bill and I got on pretty well with them all, despite us both being very evangelistic and trying to get them all converted.

During our time there, we did actually see two young fellows become Christians, which we were very excited about. Regularly, there must have been four or five Christians working there and in break times in the canteen, we would all sit at one table reading our Bibles and discussing Christian things. I don't know what the other workers must have thought of us, maybe "religious head cases," maybe we were all just a bit intense.

Enjoying being a Christian

Besides going to our Friday night Bible study at the Powers' house, we also got to hear of another group in Kings Heath run by a chap called Dan Wooding with his wife Norma. Dan was the son of a retired missionary, who with his wife lived downstairs in the house in Featherstone Rd, while Dan and Norma had the upstairs. They held a meeting for young people on a Wednesday night which we joined along with others from the Friday night group, and we later became known as the Messengers because we'd started going out telling others of the good things God had done for us. It may sound strange, but the quite shy farm worker I had been formerly was now going into pubs and clubs singing and telling folk about how God can change lives through Jesus Christ.

I had been finding out a bit more about OM (Operation Mobilization) and decided I would go with them again in the following summer. I was accepted to join them for the month of August. I just needed to find another job for three months to keep me going. It must have been around this time that our first little car was past its sell-by date; it had holes in the bodywork and floor as well as mechanical problems. Our next-door neighbour in the cottages was selling his Ford Zephyr Zodiac for £35. I must have had some money then because I bought it. It was a bit old and I ended up re-painting it dark blue with a white top after I had filled the holes in the bodywork.

It had bench seats front and back (though still no seat belts), column gear change and a two litre, six cylinder engine. This was a great car for us. We were able to give lifts to seven of the group in this car much more comfortably, and what a beautiful car it was to drive.

There was a lot of other things going on at this time. The Messengers, led by Dan, were getting quite well known in Birmingham and we were getting invites to visit other churches and share our stories of what God was doing in our lives, when Dan would often preach.
With another group called The Blue Ribands (not sure why), we found an old empty bank in Birmingham city centre which we were given permission to use. On Sunday nights we started a 9.00 o'clock meeting which we called 'Late Night Special' and invited anyone we could find on the streets in the city to come in and hear some gospel groups sing. There was also a message about Jesus, and they could have a coffee with us and a chat. All of us young people converged there after our own church

services and stayed till late. Needless to say, we had some pretty exciting times, including one night a young man going up on stage carrying a chair with which he threatened to hit Dan, who was preaching, over the head. Thankfully someone followed him up there and relieved him of the chair before he could do any harm.

Probably the most exciting thing at this time took place after Dan Wooding, the leader of The Messengers, met Dave Wilkinson from America.

He writes of this time:
> I had met up with an American called David Wilkinson at a local television studio in Birmingham. Like many of us, I had read his best-selling book, "The Cross and the Switchblade," which he wrote in 1962 with John and Elizabeth Sherrill, and told his inspiring story of how, as a young preacher from the Pennsylvania hills, he travelled to New York City and was able to influence troubled teenagers, mainly gang members, with his inspirational message, and he helped many of them give their lives to Christ and come off drugs.
>
> On hearing that David Wilkerson was going to appear as a guest on a TV show in the city, I drove over there and, as Wilkerson emerged from the studio, I introduced myself and offered to drive him back to his hotel. During that drive into the city centre, I was able to share with him about how our team, which was based at the Sparkbrook Mission, where my father, the Rev. Alfred Wooding, was the pastor, had begun visiting drug addicts being treated at All Saints Hospital in the Winston Green area of the city, but we

had discovered that once they left the hospital, many of them went straight back onto drugs.

Some local businessmen and a pastor have found a run-down place called Hill Farm, in the Worcestershire countryside and are helping to buy it so we can start a rehabilitation centre," I told Wilkerson. "What do you think?"

The Rev. Wilkerson looked doubtful and warned me, 'Are you sure that God has guided you into this work, as it is very difficult, with many disappointments?' After I reassured him that I did feel that God was in this, he wished me God's richest blessing in this new work.

Soon, we were spending all our spare time in converting the property into what turned out to be Europe's first drug rehabilitation farm. One of our team, Terry Cambridge, was a bricklayer, and he worked full time in bringing the farm into a liveable state. Once all the work was completed, the farm looked really nice, and my wife Norma and I along with our two-and-a-half-year-old son, Andrew moved into Hill Farm to become its first wardens. (Our second son, Peter, came along later).

However, we were in for a bit of a shock, for once we had done all the work, we were told by one of the businessmen that the team were no longer needed, and Norma and I were to be left alone to run the place. That was a daunting task, as the addicts from All Saints Hospital soon filled up the farm. It was particularly difficult for Norma, who was told by the same man that she had to do all the cooking and cleaning, and the addicts were not allowed to help her. 'They,' he said, 'have to take care of the farm,' which was now well stocked with chickens.

There were also huge differences between the way we wanted to run the farm, and the philosophy of some of the businessmen. We wanted the farm to be a warm, friendly and loving home for the addicts, many of whom had never experienced being part of a loving family, while some of the businessmen wanted it to be run in a military style, with strict discipline enforced by us.

Dan later told me, "We found we couldn't agree with that, and also Norma became really ill with all the work she was expected to do." So, after a few months, Dan and Norma were forced to resign, and another couple took over the running of Hill Farm. Eventually, it closed down, and Dan chronicled all that had happened in his first book, "Junkies are People Too" (published by Scripture Union).

It wasn't all bad for Dan, however, as after leaving the farm, he again became the leader of the Messengers. A few years later, he was able to start a new career in journalism, beginning in 1968 when he was given a job with *The Christian*, the Billy Graham-owned UK newspaper, and the whole family, which now included Peter, moved to London. Eventually, Dan worked for two of the UK's top-circulation newspapers, and did interviews for the BBC and LBC, the main commercial talk radio station in London.

Back to Europe again with OM

The following summer, there were several of the Messengers planning to go on OM including myself and Grace, who somehow managed to get five weeks off work to go. Once more I gave in my notice and left my job to go back to Zavenem for the week's preparation conference. I had learned an important lesson from my previous time with OM, so on this occasion I took an air bed and had many comfortable nights' sleep.

At the end of a busy but enjoyable preparation week we were all ready to go to our places of ministry. I had decided to go to Italy again and this time went with a group heading for a town called Padova, where we had been invited to work with a church on the outskirts of the city.

Our journey down also had a big difference for me this time as I had passed the lorry driving test and was one of the three drivers, so I had a much better view of the passing countryside from the cab. We had a strict driving regime between us, four hours on, eight off during daytime and two hours each during the night, travelling at a steady but slow 40 miles per hour. We eventually reached our destination safely.

Once there we set up camp in the gardens behind the church which had invited us to work in their area. There was one tent for about six of us fellows and another for around eight girls. Some of those who had travelled down in another truck went elsewhere and I was left as the driver for our team in Padova. These old trucks needed a bit of skill to drive them; there was no synchromesh on the gears, so you had to double de-clutch for changing up and changing down. If it wasn't done properly you heard some pretty awful crashing noises from the gearbox! But I really found them a joy to drive.

An OM truck like one I drove in Padova

Every day I did the driving for the team, except for one day when I had to give it a miss. We were about to get going when I felt suddenly a little bit off in my tummy and had to make a quick dash for the toilet. I didn't feel too well after that and had to go and have a lie down, so our reserve driver had to take over for that day. I was back to normal next day and judging from some of the comments from the team they were glad to have me back. The reserve driver confessed later that he also was glad I was okay again as he had not enjoyed his experience either.

On one of our days off, one of the families from the church decided they would like to invite us all to their house for a meal. On arrival, we were all seated round a large table and the first course was served to us, just a portion of pasta, followed by salad, followed by a small square of something

I had never had before, followed by several other courses. After an hour and ten courses later, we were relieved when they stopped producing food, but that was only a short interval while they washed the plates, then the meal resumed with another five courses. Needless to say, after nearly two hours we were well and truly full to overflowing. I can definitely say it was a meal I will never forget and has never been repeated in the whole of my lifetime.

One other memory stands out. It was decided we would have a day out at the seaside. It must have been perhaps a bit more than an hour's journey for us in our old van. We had a great day: it was sunny, the sea was warm, we had a lovely picnic and relaxed. In the afternoon, a bit of a breeze came up, so I sat in the sun to stay warm till it was time to pack up. The journey back was quite a slow one as everyone seemed to have decided to go home at the same time and we were stuck in long traffic jams. When we finally got back to camp, I found it extremely difficult to get out of the driving seat; it was as if all my skin had gone really tight and seized up. All I could manage was to get to my bed and cover myself with cream and go to sleep. Fortunately, in the morning I found there were no after-effects and I was able to continue as normal.

Padova is a great place to visit. From what I can remember, in the centre there was a road which I often drove along, which went round the outside of a circular water canal which had statues either side and a grassed area in the middle and was surrounded by some beautiful old buildings. I would love to go back there again after nearly fifty years to see what it like today.

After our four weeks in Italy, sadly we once more commenced our slow journey back to the base in Belgium, which must have taken about two days non-stop driving. Once back in Zavenem there was just time to say goodbye to friends and then we went onwards to the overnight ferry where we slept out on the deck in our sleeping bags again, and then home by coach.

It was nice to see Grace again (she'd been in a different team) and we had a lot to share with our friends in the Messengers when we met up with them. It was good to be home – I think mum had really missed us and was glad to have us back again. While I had been away, I had been considering what I should be doing with my life. One thought I had was to go on a two-year OM mission, but in the end I felt it was right for me to stay at home with mum and get a job again. As it happened, it wasn't long before Mr Rushton at the medical warehouse heard I needed a job and he very kindly made a position for me as stock controller in the warehouse. I quite enjoyed this job as it held a certain amount of responsibility, and I felt gratified that Mr Rushton had confidence in me to do it. The only difficulty I had was that many of the medicines and drugs were known by their Latin names and were hard to pronounce and remember.

This job only lasted for a short while though, because a vacancy came up for a delivery driver and I was asked if I would fill this post. I quite enjoyed driving, so leapt at the chance. My job now entailed joining the other drivers first thing in the morning to pack the orders and load them in the right order into the van, then setting off on the delivery run, delivering to chemists, doctors' surgeries, factories and small businesses.

The delivery run I was given was quite a long one covering a large area of the West Midlands, starting off in the so-called Black Country going through West Bromwich, Dudley, Wolverhampton, and sometimes up as far as Staffordshire. Initially, I found it hard to get round everywhere in one day and had to drive quite fast. This was a costly mistake when I was caught in a speed trap in my first week – back then they caught you by using a big black box in the back window of a car. It should have been easily spotted but I missed it.

As I got to know the area better, it became a pleasant day out which I enjoyed, particularly the first part going through the Black Country where I admired the architecture of the old buildings and the many small Wesleyan Methodist chapels which dated back to the time when John Wesley travelled round Britain preaching the gospel in the 1700s. It's said he clocked up around 4000 miles a year on horseback preaching to great crowds of folk in the open air in towns and villages!

Amongst some of the memories which stand out was a visit to an iron foundry where the sound of the machinery was so loud you couldn't hear anything that people said to you. I must have spent around 20 minutes asking folk where the infirmary was and trying, rather unsuccessfully, to lip read their answers.

At another small factory, when turning around in their yard after making the delivery, one of the back wheels went down a large hole in the ground. As I sat there wondering what to do, a big burly Black Country fellow ambled over and said, "Ah, you'm stuck, are you'm?" and without another word, he lifted the van and pushed it out. I think that was typical of these big-hearted Black Country chaps, they were a delight to meet.

I must have done around six months on the deliveries when I was approached again by Mr Rushton, who wanted me to do another job in the warehouse. This time I was promoted to quite a responsible job of checking the orders to make sure they were correct before being packed for delivery, i.e. they were the right drugs, right strength, and right amount. They were then double-checked by another person (often Mr Rushton himself) to make sure no mistakes were ever made. The money still wasn't great, but at least I felt pretty good walking around in my white coat looking important.

A big change in my life

Now there's another part to the story at this time which was eventually going to have a profound effect on my life. During the early years of my Christian life, I had gone with some of my friends to various Christian conferences in different parts of the country and had the privilege of hearing some great preachers of that time – Major Ian Thomas, Arthur Wallace, George Verger, to name but a few. Then it happened that Ron and Jan had an invite to a conference on the Wirral, Merseyside, at a place called the Longcroft. An Anglican vicar, the Rev Norman Meeten and an ex-Baptist minister, Pastor GW North had been preaching and teaching at this conference. Ron and Jan were so excited and moved by all they had seen and heard related it to us all in our group. We felt we just had to go along to the next conference which, as we discovered, was held on the next bank holiday.

So it was, several weeks later a small group of us from the circles we were involved in, set off in our old cars up the A41 (it was before the M6 was finished) to see for ourselves what it was all about. When we eventually got there after some hours of driving, we found the conference was being held in a beautiful large country house.

The Longcroft had been the family home of the Milners, a rich family who had a factory making the famous 'Milner Safes'. When Mr and Mrs Milner had died it had been left to one of the daughters who was a missionary in India, and when she returned to England she decided to give it over to a trust to be used for Christian ministry.

We were rather overawed by the whole thing, the venue, the openness and freedom of worship, the sense of the presence of God and the preaching. We had a wonderful weekend, making some great new friends and sang lots of hymns, which they did with great enthusiasm.

We also took a trip to New Brighton where we indulged ourselves with some fish and chips for we discovered that although the spiritual food was wonderful, the physical food was a bit sparse – not that we minded too much, there wasn't a charge for the conference and the folk there just shared what they had with everyone.

The conference was organised by a house church that had just recently come into being in Liverpool. As I understand it, it had begun when several young men started asking the Rev Norman Meeten (then the Curate of St Saviour's Church in Toxteth) some very challenging questions which he was having difficulty answering. Because they had a desire to know God in a deeper way, they decided to rent an old house together in Queens Rd, Anfield, where they started having regular meetings together. News of these meetings spread very rapidly throughout Liverpool and before long the house was packed out with folk from different backgrounds and ages all seeking a deeper walk with God. This was the start of a new church. I only ever visited this house once on the way to going to the Longcroft and I don't remember much about it.

When this house proved to be too small, they began looking around for a bigger venue. Eventually a near-derelict house in Devonshire Rd, Toxteth was discovered. They didn't have any money at the time to buy a house but nevertheless they approached the estate agents concerning it. It was selling for offers around £4,000. Rev Meeten recalls how after prayer he felt led to make an offer of £2,000. The estate agents were very dubious about this amount but passed the offer on to the owner of the property and were very surprised when it was accepted. All that was needed now was to actually have the money to buy it. The contracts went through though and amazingly, by the due date for the money to be paid, it had all come in through gifts and was paid in full.

The house was in a terrible condition. I'm told the basement was full of sewage and the place needed renovating from top to bottom, but work was begun by volunteers and soon Norman Meeten and his new wife Jenny were able to move into the top flat, although it wasn't entirely suitable for a newly married couple – initially there were no doors on the flat!

The house was a Victorian three-storey building and it

would have been a beautiful property in its day. Liverpool had been a very rich city in years gone by and had lots of these majestic beautiful houses, but many had been sadly neglected and were often stripped and converted into flats; some were even allowed to become derelict.

Undeterred by its awful condition, work was started by volunteers in the church. With their hard work it was slowly transformed into something near its former glory. Part of the early work done was to knock the two large lounges on the ground floor into one room. This became the meeting room for the new church, large enough to hold upwards of two hundred people, much needed at this point as the church continued to grow rapidly.

Around this time for various reasons the Longcroft could no longer be used for conferences and so the Devonshire Rd house became the venue. Our group continued to come up from the Midlands for these conferences, sometimes up to 15 of us went, and we became known as the Birmingham folk. We were all still fairly young Christians and these conferences had quite a valuable impact on our lives. We also had a lot of fun together. One of the highlights was still to go over to New Brighton for fish and chips. The Mersey ferry in those days went all the way up to New Brighton and it made it a very pleasant trip out for us all.

We have many enduring memories of these visits to Liverpool; we made many friends, both in Liverpool and other parts of the country which remain to this day. At the time of writing this (2017), it is now fifty years ago since it happened and the house church in Devonshire Rd is still going strongly.

We also had a few adventures on our journeys to and from Liverpool in our old cars. On one occasion, at the last meeting of a conference, some of our folk needed to leave to go home before the end of the meeting, as they had to be up early for work on the following morning. It was agreed that the smaller group would take my car, the Zephyr Zodiac, as with its large engine it would get them back quicker, and I would take the larger group in the minibus later in the evening at the end of the conference.

Our team minibus, it should be pointed out, was pretty old, didn't go very fast and you had to turn the steering wheel back and forth constantly to keep going in a straight line as there was a bit of play in the steering.

We were making steady progress on our journey, when around 1 o'clock in the morning as I was getting near to Stafford on the M6 doing about 60 mph top speed, I noticed out the corner of my eye as we flashed past in the dark, the white top of a car that looked strangely like mine, and heard some people screaming. We pulled over quickly onto the hard shoulder and discovered it <u>was</u> my car and that the engine had blown. Of course this was in the days before mobile phones and none of us could afford the RAC or AA, so all they could do was push the car down the hard shoulder in the hope of coming off the motorway and finding some help, while keeping an eye open in the hope of seeing me come past as well.

As we considered the situation, we were still not sure what we could do. The police had stopped earlier and told them they should not be pushing the car on the hard shoulder. However, when we looked at where we were, we saw there was an exit off the motorway not too far in the distance, so with all the folk in the bus piling out to help, we quickly succeeded in getting the Zephyr off the motorway and onto a lay-by on the main road. As we all stood there considering what we to do next, a lorry driver strolled up with a rope in his hand asking if it would help us. With grateful thanks, we tied my car to the back of the minibus and were soon on our way again, albeit at a much slower pace, and we eventually got home about 5.00 in the morning, which was a bit hard for those going to work, I guess, but we were all grateful to God for answered prayer and that we had all got back safely.

That could have been the end of my lovely Zephyr Zodiac, but I was able to find another engine in a scrap yard for £10 and somehow managed to change it myself. This engine, however, was worse than the last one, using oil by the gallon so, reluctantly we scrapped the car, and between us (Grace and me) we found an old (about 1953) VW Beetle for £70. We so loved this car and it just kept going and going, despite the engine bearings rattling a bit. We travelled extensively all over the country and had it for quite a few years.

There was a strange custom amongst VW owners in those days: whenever you saw another one go past, you had to raise a hand and give a little wave to them, which was quite fun. It was a smaller car than the Zephyr but we still managed to fit four or five friends in when we were going places, though there was not much space for luggage.

Sometime later, Grace and I decided it would be a nice idea to have a caravanette. After a short search we found a lovely one, Volkswagen again, Mark 1 with the split front window, being sold for £400. It sounds cheap compared with today's prices, but back then it was a lot more money than we could afford, so we enquired about getting a loan. As we didn't have bank accounts, we needed someone to be a guarantor to get the van on HP, so I went to see Uncle Arthur who agreed to this arrangement. As an afterthought, he asked if we wouldn't rather that he just lent us the money and then we could pay it back bit by bit as we were able; we wouldn't have to pay interest on the loan that way. We gratefully accepted his kind offer and thankfully, with a few generous gifts for some of our friends, we were able to repay him quite quickly.

We now became the proud owners of a beautiful Devon conversion VW caravanette. We so enjoyed our new vehicle, using it to give lifts to lots of our friends. We also took Mum on holiday to Scotland in it, visiting our relatives and friends in Alexandria, near Loch Lomond. It was enjoyable as we'd not seen them for a long time, then we toured up through Fort William and followed the road alongside Loch Ness as far as Inverness, then went back down to St Andrews and Edinburgh.

VW Caravanette just like ours – it was well used and we loved it so much.

During these early years from the time that we had become Christians a lot of things started to change for me. The first leaders of the Messengers moved on. As already mentioned, Dan had gone to London, some of the other leading fellows left to go to Bible College, including Clive, the minibus driver, who went to the Glasgow Bible Institute and others went to Birmingham Bible Institute. John Miles left to go to India for 2 years with OM. Before leaving, he and Grace, who had been going out together for a while, got engaged. With a shortage of other chaps now to take over, it fell to me to become the new leader of a much smaller but still enthusiastic group. I was not much of a speaker or preacher, but we still had many happy times together.

Now I come to 1970. At this point in my life, I started keeping a diary, which is good because my memory of all the things which happened is a bit vague, all these years later. The diary tells me that on the 23rd January I got engaged to M, whom I had been courting for several months and we had a party. On 3rd February, coming home from work, the caravanette engine seized up just as I reached home. We were now for a while car-less. We still had the VW Beetle but it was also sitting in our drive with a fault and we had no money to repair either vehicle. We had to resign ourselves to travelling on buses again, which was not very nice as it was a cold wet winter, as I remember.

I found just at this time a neighbour was selling an old Beetle for £10. It had a loose flywheel on the engine and I wondered if I could mend that then put the engine from it into our car. However, when I managed to get the engine out I found I didn't have the tools to fix it, so now we had three VWs sitting dormant on our drive – "Hmm, what to do now?" I thought. 1950s VW beetle

For a while, my relationship with M went well, but slowly the differences between us began to tell and things started to get difficult. About that time, Pastor North came to Birmingham on a preaching tour, so we both went separately to see him and ask for advice. He wisely recommended we have a period apart to consider and pray about our relationship and our future. I had seen another couple do this in our group who had not been sure of their relationship, and it had ended very happily for them, so I thought it might work out for us the same way.

After some thought, I decided it would be best if I should go away for a while. It was easier for me to leave the job that I was in than for her to do so, so I wrote to the Rev Norman Meeten in Liverpool asking if I could stay in the fellowship house for a short period, explaining the situation to him. He wrote back confirming they would be happy to have me, and he recommended that I get a job for the time I would be spending in Liverpool. So it was that in April 1970 I gave in my notice to Mr Rushton at the medical warehouse, said goodbye to mum and Grace, and set off for Toxteth with the intention of just staying there for around three months before returning home.

Some friends, Paul and Mary, gave me a lift up to Liverpool with my suitcase. I was twenty-three and although I had been abroad for a few weeks at a time, this was the first time I had ever moved away from home properly. Even though it was for a limited period, I still found it a bit of an emotional upheaval. It was made a little easier though as I already knew quite a few folks living in the fellowship house at that time, including a good friend Brett from our group in Birmingham, who had already moved to Liverpool to start a new job with ICI in Runcorn. We ended up after a while sharing a room together.

One of the other chaps who lived in the house at that time, Peter Lock, had a job in Plessey's, a factory that produced telecommunication equipment. He suggested I apply for a job there, so one Monday morning I went along, and was given a simple test of putting round pegs into holes in the right order within a time limit. I managed it and was given a job, which I started on the following Monday – how easy it was to get jobs in those days!

I had a week to have a look around and get acclimatised to my new surroundings. This included learning how Liverpudlians spoke and the interpretation of different words they used, like 'sound' meaning something was good, and 'made up' meaning being pleased, happy with yourself for some reason. A favourite phrase back then was 'to catch a crozy to wizi hozi', which meant 'to catch a Crosville bus to Whiston Hospital'. I remember on one of those days when out walking and exploring the locality, a man shouted over to me, "Hey Jimmy, do you have the time?" I thought to myself, "How do they know my name up here?" – not realising that 'Jimmy' was the equivalent of 'mate'.

On the following Monday, I set off early for my first day in my new job. A short bus ride and a walk through a park led me along with several hundred other men and women in through the factory gates. I joined a group of around ten other men in the training department, where we were to receive some general instruction on the type of work we could be doing. We were all seated around a large workbench, and a rather well-built man in a brown overall gave us a lesson in how to do wiring etc. Much of the time, however, was taken up with chatting amongst ourselves and getting to know one another.

Next day, one of the lads said to me, "You seem a bit different to the rest of us, what is it?" "Oh, I'm a Christian," I confessed. And that was the beginning of my having to explain, for the foreseeable future, how I came to be a Christian, what it meant to me and what the Christian faith is all about.

For the first few days there wasn't much for us to do, so I decided to have a bit of fun with my new workmates. In the middle of the workbench I had noticed a couple of small transformers, and as I knew a little about electronics from my school days, I thought I'd make a shock machine with one of them. Once finished, and while the tutor was in his little office, I proceeded to tell the lads of my experiment and got them all to hold hands around the table. The ones at each end were to hold one of the wires from the transformer in their free hand. I then proceeded to make a connection, which sent a small charge through all them causing them all to throw their hands up in the air and burst out laughing. Wouldn't you just know it, the tutor happened to look out of his window just at that point to see all the hands shoot up! He never said anything though.

It was decided we were to go to work in the department that made **universal selectors.** This was before the discovery of the silicon chip, so devices like these were part electronic and part mechanical. They were designed to connect you to a free phone line when you lifted your phone to make a call. I soon learned the part I had to play in the construction of these devices, and then was sent to department 22 which produced them.

I was one of a group of lads who made the final fine adjustments to make sure the selectors worked properly. Once finished, we put our own identifying stamp on and added them to the tray of finished work which eventually went to an examiner to check and add his pass mark. We had a quota to fulfil each day, I think it was about eighty, that is, ten an hour, so you had to work pretty quickly to keep up.

You could say that it was quite a boring job doing the same thing eight hours a day, five days a week, but actually I enjoyed it. It was partly the challenge of trying to get every one right and not get any rejects returned, but also I enjoyed working with the group of lads on my workbench, all were Scousers, apart from two (one from Wales and the other from Iran). The days passed quickly with all the talk and banter that Liverpudlians are renowned for – part of it at my expense, as I was the only Christian in the workshop, apart from the manager of unit 22, who I eventually discovered was also a Christian and an elder of a local church. He started having me in to his office every now and then to have little chats with me about our common faith. I'm not sure what the lads thought of me being called to the office, they probably thought that I was in trouble again over my struggles to fulfil my daily quotas, mainly due to my fixation to do a perfect job and my inability to talk and work at the same time.

I made one friend during my time there, the lad from Iran. His name was Adnan, but everybody called him Ted. He was about eighteen years old and had come over to study in college in Liverpool. Unfortunately, he told me, the high life of the city had been too much of a temptation for him and he wasted his college fees on having a good time. He gave his family back home in Iran a sob story as to how he lost all his money, and managed to persuade them to send more, but when this had all gone also in the same way, the family suspected his untruthfulness and refused to send him any more money, telling him he was on his own to sort it out. That is how he ended up working in Plessey's.

We got on well and often had lunch together in the factory canteen, and on one occasion he came along for a meal with me in the church house which was interesting, as he was a Muslim. During those early weeks, I kept in touch with M by phone and letters and I often went down to Birmingham at weekends to see her (and my mum as well, of course). Sadly, things between us didn't seem to be getting any better, and by the middle of summer, we arranged to meet together with Norman Meeten. After talking it through sadly with tears, but by mutual consent, we broke off our engagement and separated. I was not at all sure what to do now, but thought for the time being it was best for me to remain in Liverpool. I continued working in Plessey's and living in the church house (fondly known as The House to the folk in Liverpool) and I generally got more involved in all that was going on there.

By September John Miles had returned from India and with his help I got the engine out of the caravanette and took it down to the OM garage in London where they maintained all their vehicles. They stripped the engine down and repaired it for us. We gave them the other old Beetle I had bought for £10 as payment for the work they did for us. I often wonder what happened to that car, because what we didn't realise then was that it was actually a very old and rare model with a rear split window. Today they are worth many thousands of pounds!

We managed to get our first Beetle on the Road again and I took it back to use up in Liverpool; John and Grace kept the Caravanette once it was fixed. It was nice to be mobile again and I continued to travel down at weekends to see mum, often picking up a hitchhiker on the way to have someone to chat to and break the monotony. (I'm not sure that I would do that today.)

On a sunny day in October, I went down to Birmingham for the weekend and had the pleasure of giving Grace away in marriage to John Miles. It was a lovely wedding with lots of our friends and family there to witness and enjoy it. Afterwards, at the reception, I had the job of giving a speech in the place of our dad. (Apparently, I went on a bit, so I was told afterwards.) On their return from honeymoon, Grace and John moved into the little cottage next to mum. It was their first home for a short time before they bought a more modern house just a short distance away. I returned to Liverpool after their wedding with a deeper feeling that Birmingham was no longer my home, and that the time had come for me to move on with my life. I was not sure in which direction, but felt I was on the edge of something new.

At work in Plessey's, there was some unrest amongst the workforce, the union was pressing the management for an increase in wages. As I was not in the union, the rep in our department started pressurising me a bit to join – not that I was against being in the union, I think it was just that I was content with the wage I was on and felt relatively well off. I suppose for those in the workforce who were married it might have been different. Anyway, the pressure increased, and in the end I agreed with the proviso that I could speak to our department in a lunch hour and explain from a Christian point of view how I felt about it all. A few days later, after eating my sandwiches rather hurriedly, I stood in a corner of our workshop with a few folks around me, with my Bible in my hand and read from Luke's Gospel, chapter 12, the following words:

> 22 Then He said to His disciples, "Therefore I say to you, do not worry about your life, what you will eat; nor about the body, what you will put on.
> 23 Life is more than food, and the body is more

than clothing.

24 Consider the ravens, for they neither sow nor reap, which have neither storehouse nor barn; and God feeds them. Of how much more value are you than the birds?

As I read these words rather nervously, the group rapidly grew in number, many asking questions which were difficult to answer as there were so many of them, it was almost as if they'd never heard the Bible being read to them before. When the bell went for us to resume work, the union rep commented to me that he thought I'd made many friends that day. Funnily enough, though, I never got to join the union after all as other events overtook me very quickly!

I had been residing now in Liverpool for nearly nine months and I began to reflect on my situation. John and Grace were married and living in the small cottage next to mum, so she was cared for now and I felt free from home ties. The Messengers had dwindled to quite a small number and on his return from India, John had felt to close it down, so I no longer had any responsibilities towards them. I felt I had gained my independence as a free single man and that I should now consider the future and what I would like to do. Three possibilities came into my mind where I thought I could be of some use. Firstly, I had heard that there was a Christian bookshop in Kendal up in the Lake District, and they were in need of someone to join them to help in the work. I didn't know anything about book shops but thought I could give it a go. Next, I thought of my good friend Clive, whom a few years previously we had taken up to Glasgow. He'd now finished at Bible college and had stayed on in the city, involved with a church doing street work, helping down and outs, alcoholics and that sort of thing. Maybe I could go and be of use there (I quite liked the idea of being back in Scotland). And then lastly, right here where I was living in the church house, I'd noticed that although a great deal of work in renovating the building had been done, there was still an awful lot more to do, particularly painting and decorating.

According to my 1970 diary, on 17th December I approached the leading elders of the church to discuss my thoughts. They felt that I should come to work in the house for a short period of time and be involved with the day-to-day running of it and do any work on it that was deemed necessary. The condition of working there was that, along with the others who also worked there full-time, I would have free board and lodging, but had to trust God to supply all my other needs. The week before Christmas, I went to see my boss in workshop 22 to hand in my notice and tell him of my plans for the future. I was somewhat surprised by his response. He was most concerned for me that I was moving to a job where there was no pay and asked how I would manage. Unfortunately, I never had the opportunity to see him again to tell him of the wonderful time I had working there for the next four years, how I managed to live, run the VW van, and travel extensively throughout England, Scotland and Wales, and even abroad, all without pay.

My work in the house initially was mostly practical, decorating (of which there was still a lot to do in the three-storey house) and maintenance. There were two other fellows also working there, a young man, Peter Gray, and an older gentleman, David Wetherley, who made everyone who entered that house feel so special and loved. They did all the carpentry and building work. I now swopped vehicles with John and Grace and had the VW caravanette in Liverpool, so I was often asked to help with getting things needed for the house, to move stuff for people in the church or to give lifts to people when necessary.

One of my first assignments was to help a young lady and her mother. Norman Meeten had promised to give them a lift to a doctor's appointment but at the last minute he was needed elsewhere, so I was asked to step in and give them a lift. Little did I know that the young lady, Jean, was destined to become my wife four years later.

After a short while, Norman Meeten moved on from being the pastor of the church and two younger men came to take his place as leaders and pastors: Fred Tomlinson with his wife Sheila, and John Valentine. I became quite involved with them over the years, both in the work of the house and sometimes travelling with them in the UK and abroad. We had some wonderful times and great adventures on some of these trips, about which I could write another book (maybe a job for another time).

Over my four years working in the house for the church, I often felt quite lonely, despite the kindness and love of so many in the church. I guess I had the natural longing to find the right girl who I could love and spend the rest of my life with. There were lots of lovely young ladies in the church at that time, but I just didn't seem to be able to find the one that was for me. Over the four years I worked in the house, many of the young people in the church got engaged and then married. In one summer, there were five weddings on five consecutive weekends! We were all pretty exhausted at the end of it. I seem to remember I was an usher at every one of them. I was beginning to wonder if it would ever happen to me.

Back to Gracie's account

On the day when I raised my hand and gave myself over to Christ, I realised that I had to say 'goodbye' to that non-Christian boyfriend. So I sat down and wrote him a letter to tell him that I had heard God calling me and had given myself fully into His hands, therefore I could not see him any more – I told him I hoped and would pray that he too would find the peace and joy that could only be found in God. (He soon found another girlfriend!) Back home again I went to our church and told the 2 lads who were also struggling with the lack of life in the church what had happened to me. One of the 2 lads – Ronnie- had just been on a mission to Spain, and he was thrilled to hear my news, and then told me of the way God had blessed him on his trip to Spain. During the following week, I felt very frustrated, - I couldn't see how I could grow spiritually if I stayed in this church. By Friday I was very anxious and upstairs in my bedroom I got on my knees and prayed - 'Lord, I cannot see how I can grow without some help – please send someone round to help me tonight!' (A tall order, I thought). Half an hour later my friend Ronnie arrived saying 'I've just heard about a young couple called John and Margaret who open their house to young people on Fridays, for Bible Study and prayer – would you like to go?' Would I? – I knew this was the answer to my prayer so jumped into Ronnie's car and we shot off to Bordesley Green.

That evening was the beginning of a new chapter in my life. I got lots of encouragement and good teaching and made some lovely new friends, who all had the heart to serve God and grow into all that He wanted for them. We met each Friday night and were very challenged and encouraged by the lovely couple, John and Margaret, who had opened their house to quite a large group of young people. Shortly after this, I decided to leave the Baptist Church as I was very excited to be part of this other group of like-minded young people who felt God was calling them to serve Him wholeheartedly.

The Messengers Evangelistic Team (Just a few of them)

One of our new friends at the Friday Bible Study told us about a team of young people who were doing evangelism at weekends. The team were called 'The Messengers'. Excitedly most of the young people from the Friday group decided to join 'The Messengers'.
We started going to the team leader's house on Sunday afternoons and joined his Dad's church – Sparkbrook Mission. Dan and Norma Wooding had been running 'The Messengers' for a while, and the team would meet at the

church on Saturday evenings for prayer, then would go out on the streets of Balsall Heath to sing and chat to people in the pubs, or go to coffee bars to chat to coffee drinkers. Some Saturdays the team would go to the City Centre to have an open-air meeting in the Bull Ring, then talk to people who gathered to listen. I suppose people were more open to listen in those days than nowadays. We often had long discussions with young and even older people.

We were sometimes a little naïve though, and one evening I found myself walking through Moseley with one of our male team members and a drunk man who we wanted to talk further with. My fellow team member was in conversation with this drunk man, and I happened to add something to what he'd said – the drunk man turned to me in anger, raised his fist and told me if I said another word he'd punch me in the face. Needless to say, I shut up after that!

We just loved these opportunities and each weekend would find us doing evangelism in the city centre or in Balsall Heath on Saturday evenings, then on Sundays, we'd go to Sparkbrook Mission in the morning, Bible Study in Featherstone Road on Sunday afternoons, and often went to take meetings at different churches in the evening. Around this time, my cousin Dee had asked me if I would like to buy her car an Austin A30 – for £25!!! I loved the little car but it was some years before I managed to pass my test. I took 5 driving tests before I passed – oops!

My brother Jim had started to come to the Friday Bible Study also, and he had passed his test, so we eventually scrapped my little car which was wearing out, and bought a car together from another of my cousins – for £30 - so we were able to get out and about easier.

I had decided to take my driving test in Redditch as I thought it would be easier than the suburbs of Birmingham. But on my first test, I realised that there were lots of steep hills, and sharp bends (which the examiners loved to take me to for hill starts and reversing! Needless to say, I failed my test, but the examiner I had was truly vile! He sat glaring at me, then would sigh loudly and tut when I did anything wrong – so I became more and more distracted and eventually so stressed that I stopped at a green light!!!!

My next test was even worse – people and dogs stepped out in the road in front of me, and I ended up going too slow and failed again! I then got so nervous and stressed and gave up driving and let Jimmy drive me around everywhere.

Many years later I eventually tried again at Redditch and still couldn't pass! I eventually decided to shift to another test centre – at the Maypole and found that the route was so much easier than Redditch. But I always seemed to get a very grumpy, severe-looking examiner which put me off before I started.

Eventually, on my 5th test, I passed! (not before the examiner shouted at me and told me I was a blithering idiot!) However, my driving instructor told me that he knew I'd passed because that examiner would shout at all those he passed, to try and stop them becoming too cocky!!

Someone on our team told us about a place in the Wirral that held conferences over New Year weekend, Easter weekend and August Bank holiday weekend. Apparently, the speakers were very powerful and people were being very blessed and challenged. A group of us decided to go, as it was very cheap to stay in the big old house in the Wirral – groups of girls in one room in sleeping bags, and boys in other rooms. So Jim and I and quite a few of the team went up to the Wirral for one particular weekend. The speakers were unknown to us – Norman Meeten, George North and Dave Wetherly.

We all were welcomed to the house, given a spot in the rooms for our sleeping bags, and went into the first meeting. These conferences were inspiring and very challenging for us and we learnt so much. In fact, many people feel that these conferences were the start of a revival movement and the start of house churches.

We sat in long meetings, sang long Wesley hymns and other

well-known hymns, and listened to long sermons, but we hung on every word – it was teaching that we had never heard before, and was very powerful. There was such a strong presence of God in those meetings! We learned so much and were thrilled at being there. Those organising these conferences had very little money as they charged very minimally – so we'd eat peanut butter and jam sandwiches for breakfast, lunch and dinner! But we didn't mind – and we met lots of other like-minded young people like ourselves. The folk in Liverpool and in the Wirral opened their houses to lots of young and older folk for ministry, prayer and fellowship and each New Year and Easter holidays we got into the habit of going up to Liverpool to a big house in Devonshire Road after the Wirral house became too small. After some years my brother Jim decided to go and live in Liverpool and he moved into the big house in Devonshire Road.

Back in Birmingham, one of the team bought a J2 12 seater minibus and he very generously used it to ferry all the team around, even up to Liverpool and back. His name was John Miles and he eventually became the team leader, when Dan and Norma left the team to go and run a Drug Addicts Rehabilitation Centre near Wythall.

This was an exciting development, though there were not that many drug addicts in the UK at that time, it was becoming a problem.

Dan and Norma had seen a big rundown farmhouse for sale, right in the middle of the countryside near Wythall, and they started to pray about buying this farmhouse and surrounding land. The Lord provided the deposit of £10,000 quite quickly, and it was bought, then our team would spend evenings and Saturdays at Hill Farm, starting the renovation of the farmhouse.

Some wealthy Christian businessmen had also been approached to see if they could help with the finances. Some agreed and enabled the farmhouse to be renovated and converted suitably to house young men in dormitories, with a separate flat for Dan and Norma and their 2 boys. We got to know some of the first addicts who moved in and occasionally helped out with looking after them on Saturdays. They seemed a nice bunch of young men on the surface, but despite being in the middle of the countryside where there was no shops, no bus service and no proximity to other houses, they always seemed to find a way to get bottles of cough mixture, which had certain drugs in, and often lots of these bottles would be found under their beds. I do believe that some went on to be clean and some became Christians, but some became quite a disappointment to us all. Dan and Norma worked very hard with the addicts, but eventually became very exhausted with the stress of looking after them all, on their own, so the group of wealthy businessmen who had put lots of their own money into the farm, took the project over. Dan and Norma moved on to another ministry in London.

John and I were friends but nothing more for some years, but one evening when we were in the city centre doing our 'Late Night Special' evangelistic work at St. Martins in the Bull Ring, he had been asked to give the epilogue to all the people we'd invited in, so he'd dressed up in his best suit and tie. I told him he looked very handsome in his suit –I think he was very surprised! Not long after this, he asked me out and we started going out together. Having said we were 'going out', it just meant that we went to lots of meetings, and evangelistic activities, then he would give everyone a lift home in his minibus – and he would drop me off last – then have a half hour drive home to Kitts Green. So it was a strange relationship – sometimes one of the team would ask him if they could be dropped off last, as they wanted to ask him something. Usually, he would say no, I'm glad to say. After about 3 months I felt unsure about our relationship – we didn't have any normal 'dates' together on our own, so I suppose I wasn't really getting to know him more closely. I was also very burdened for my mum who was still a widow and worried about what would happen to her if she was left on her own. So we separated in that respect, though we saw just as much of each other as before, but he didn't drop me off last any more. Not long after this John announced to the team that he had joined OM and was going to India for 2 years. We were all together at our afternoon Bible Study when he announced this. We were all surprised, and I realised how much I'd miss him. I quickly prayed and asked God to give me an opportunity to talk to John alone, if it was His will that we should be together. This seemed impossible, as he was always talking to one of the team, sorting out things, or driving everyone around. I had decided to go and visit one of the team who was ill with pneumonia that Sunday evening. John asked what plans everyone had, and most had decided to go to a church nearby. He stated that he had decided to go and visit this team member who was ill with pneumonia – so I mentioned that I had thought to do that too. Before we knew it, all the team members departed, leaving John and me on our own. I realised that God had allowed this, so I could tell him what I was thinking. So, I said to him 'John, if you want me to… I will wait for you to come back from India', (He had felt God was calling him to go with Operationr Mobilization for two yeas). He was surprised and pleased, and left for Belgium a few days later, promising to write. I hadn't realised that he had to do 9 months training in the OM garage in Zaventem before going to India!

That summer I and about 9 other team members signed up to go on an OM summer team. I and my friend Sandy together went to Austria for a month, after first spending a week in Zaventem, Belgium on the training and orientation week. John and I went for a walk together and spent time talking. I had been having a strange feeling of uncertainty again, so we both agreed to spend time praying about our future, during the month I was in Austria.

Krems on the Danube

I enjoyed our time in Austria. Our girls' team camped at the side of the river Danube, in a small town called Krems, on the beautiful river Danube. It was a lovely area and a nice campsite.

The old truck we had travelled in had been left with us, and we would have our prayer time in the evenings inside the truck. Each morning, we would have morning prayers before setting off in pairs to our allotted roads around 8 am. We would knock on the doors of houses and had learnt phrases in German to enable us to say 'Greetings in God, we have come to Austria to learn to speak German. We have some good books we would like to show you for you to buy'. Then we hoped to sell some good Christian books, and if possible have a conversation with the person who came to the door.

Of course, if they didn't speak any English, we were stuck and could only give them some literature and move on. We had not been given any money to live on during that month, so to enable us to eat and pay our campsite fees we had to sell books and use that money to buy our food.

Each morning, one of the team who had a day off would take the money from the books we'd sold the previous day, and go to the village shop to buy bread and other food for our lunch and evening meal. At the end of each day, we would find that we had managed to sell enough books to buy food for the next day. One day the person allocated to go to the shop came back and told us it was a national holiday, so all the shops were closed! The team leader was a bit shocked but found enough bread to enable us all to have a very small sandwich for our lunch. She told us we'd have to pray and ask God to provide us with food for the rest of the day. So… we all went off hoping and praying that God would provide, somehow.

Sandy and I were together again that day, and as we walked along we met a very pretty young Austrian girl, Margit, who stopped us and asked where we were from. We told her we were English and she was delighted, she had been learning English and was keen to practise what she'd learned. She invited us to come to her house to sit in the garden and eat our lunch, and we accepted eagerly. When we arrived, we sat in her garden, while she went into the house. We slowly ate our small sandwich, and still felt very hungry, after our energetic morning. Suddenly Margit came out into the garden and brought us both a lovely omelette, fruit and drink!!! We were so excited to see how the Lord had provided us with food for lunch.

Margit was a delightful young lady and we had many conversations with her in the days ahead and passed on her details to a local OM team. On arriving back at our campsite, we found most of the team had experienced similar things, and many had also been given food to bring back with them. We all rejoiced at how God had supplied our need on that day!

Later in the month, one evening we had a bit of a fright – A big American girl on the team had gone over to the building which was the communal toilets, showers, and a place for washing dishes. While doing the washing up, she saw a man creeping around the tents, with what looked like a knife in his hand. Leaving the dishes there, she rushed back to the truck, where we were all sitting preparing for our evening prayer time. She jumped into the back of the truck shouting 'There a man out there with a knife, going around the tents!' We quickly closed and locked the rear doors and sat there trying to peep out of the window and see what he was doing. She was watching through the rear windows, and suddenly said 'He's right here by the door of the truck!!!' She picked up a pot and pan and suddenly she unlocked the doors and jumped out shouting, screaming and bashing the pot and pan together making a loud noise!!!!

Thankfully, he took fright and rushed off!!! We reported it but never heard any more.

During those 4 weeks, I would spend my prayer time in the mornings, down at the side of the Danube –a beautiful spot – where I would read my Bible and pray. I started to pray each day that God would show me if it was right for John and me to be together.

One morning I prayed this and sat there just listening to see if I could hear God's voice. He did speak to me, very clearly and said 'John is mine first, you must be willing for that, then he is yours secondly!' I sat mulling this over and realised that I had been complaining that we hadn't spent much time together on our own, as there was always so many people wanting John to do things, take meetings, organise this or that, and listen to their problems. God had done something deep in me through that team experience and I realised that I wanted to put Him first in my life also. I then in my heart told God that I was willing for John to be His first and I would be second in his life. Immediately I felt a wonderful peace come over my mind and heart. It was a wonderful experience altogether, where we saw God provide for us, and protect us.

Just a week or so before we were due to return, one afternoon while we were driving home from our day of selling books, we noticed lots of army trucks driving fast towards the border and wondered what was going on. When we arrived back at our campsite, the team member who was on her day off, came rushing to us and told us that she'd heard some loud rumbling noises which went on and on. She went to the road and saw army tanks and lorries all rolling along the road, packed with soldiers.

Feeling a bit scared she went to speak to another camper nearby and asked if they knew what was going on. That person managed to speak a little English to her and told her that the radio was broadcasting the news that the Russians were threatening to come across the border and reclaim that part of Austria – which they'd apparently ruled many years ago. So the Government had called up all their soldiers and reserves and rushed them all to the border to protect our area!

Thankfully, the Russians retreated!

Our month over, we drove back to the OM base in Zaventem, and when we had a spare moment John and I sat together on our own.

I told him what God had shown me and how I had agreed with what He had shown me. He was amazed and told me that God had shown him exactly the same thing!

After John finished the 9 months in Belgium he came home briefly, we got engaged - then he was off, doing the long drive from the UK to India! It was a long 2 years… but

God kept us and we got to know each other more through lots of letters!!

John had many adventures and difficult moments, answers to prayer, and dangerous situations, which I read about in his weekly letter.

While he was in India I was kept fairly busy – at work during the week, then continuing our weekend evangelism with 'The Messengers' and our Sunday afternoon Bible Studies. The first year went by quite quickly. Halfway through the second year some of the team went off to Bible College or moved away, so things were not so busy and the time started to drag. On top of that John had mentioned in a letter that the OM leaders had suggested that if the OM ship was ready in time, perhaps he could join it – as he had engineering skills. My heart sunk a little, and I started hoping that the ship would not be 'ready-to-go' before he came home.

One day I was in the city centre on my own wandering around – when I suddenly met up with one of our 'Messenger' team members – Ruth. I must have looked a bit fed up because she asked me what was wrong. I told her that I was a bit down, wondering if John would get home in 4 months time, or whether he may be persuaded to stay on longer and go on the ship. She asked me if he would be able to leave earlier if we could raise the money to fly him home instead of the long drive back. I told her I'd ask him, but I thought he would probably say he couldn't fly back, as he would feel he had to help with the long drive back. She replied 'Well, ask him! If he can fly back a bit earlier, then I'll see if I can raise his airfare'.

I was encouraged at that and in my next letter, I asked him that question, fully expecting him to say 'No'. Reading the next letter from him, I was very surprised to see a resounding 'Yes – that would be wonderful, I am quite sick and very tired, so a flight home a little earlier would be wonderful!' I shared this with Ruth, and amazingly she soon raised the funds for his airfare home, which we sent off to OM. This meant that he came home in July, rather than September – which was great.

John just back from India

I had thought it would take a few months to get our wedding arranged, but John stated it would be good to get married in October – just 3 months away! He had some time to recover his health, then found a job to earn some money.
I had a very poor salary, and had only managed to save about £80! However, I had already bought my wedding dress – which was second hand and had belonged to my Scottish friend's sister Violet. I had gone up to Scotland a few months previously to visit my old friend, who had recently married and she showed me her wedding dress and Violet's dress which she was trying to sell. I liked the

Violets dress best and it fitted me perfectly so I bought it for £10!! During the next few weeks, the wedding plans came together and the Lord provided for us in many ways – John's brother-in-law ran a wedding service which supplied catering and a wedding car, and photographer – they gave us a good discount. My cousin's husband, Mel (who had all those years ago left me in the field with stampeding bullocks) had a florists shop – he did the flowers at cost price.

We managed to book a church hall for the reception very cheaply and asked the Pastor of Yardley Wood Tabernacle if he could marry us in his church, which he agreed to do. My mum made the bridesmaids dresses. John's parents paid for a hire car for our honeymoon as our old car had broken down. John had managed to save enough for a week in the Lake District.

My uncle offered to let us have the little cottage next to mum for us to live in for as long as we needed to – for £2 per week!! We had a lovely wedding, and everything, including the weather, was perfect. . Despite it being 17th October, we had a gloriously sunny and warm day!

On our return from the Lakes, we found a letter waiting for us – from OM – asking if we could join the OM ship which had just been bought and renovated and was ready to go! The Logos We sat down together to pray about it – wanting to be open to doing this if it was what God wanted. As we prayed, I remembered the words the Lord had given me and felt a real peace that if this was God's plan for us I was ready to do it. However, John shared with me a few days later that God had clearly shown him that it was not the Lord's plan – he had been led to read Deuteronomy 24 v 5 which said ' When a man hath taken a new wife, he shall not go out to war, neither shall he be charged with any business: but he shall be free at home one year, and shall cheer up his wife which he hath taken.'(KJ Authorised version.) So.. we took that to mean it was not God's plan for us to go, and instead, we joined the church where we were married and got involved in church activities instead. We were very blessed to be able to move into the small cottage belonging to my Uncle Arthur, - in between my Mum at 2 Fordrough Cottages, and my Granny in number 4. The cottage was ideal for young just-married couples and other young couples in our family lived there over the years. It was just one small lounge and a small kitchen downstairs and upstairs was a bathroom and 2 bedrooms. It was a godsend for us, as neither of us earned lots of money. However, we were able to buy a 6-month-old VW Beetle, using the marriage gratuity I received from my 14 years at the GPO. About 15 months later we sold it for the same price we had bought it for, to put a deposit on our first house.

Our VW Beetle

We had decided that we would try for a baby straight away – I was desperate to leave the Telephone Exchange and was 28 years old. I didn't want my children to have an 'old mother'! I also had a fear that I would take a long time to get pregnant, which some women do when they are older. To our delight, I soon was able to tell my friends at work that I was having a baby. They were very surprised at how soon it happened after our marriage and said to me 'Do we have to congratulate you or commiserate?' I was very pleased to be able to say 'Congratulate!!! I can leave work in a few months time now!'

We enjoyed being at Yardley Wood Tabernacle, though I had to apologise to the young Pastor – Ron Bailey, that each week at the prayer meeting, I would sit down, shut my eyes and go to sleep!!! He laughed and said 'That's ok – just do as your body tells you to do!'

9 months later on 31st August, I was induced at the QE Maternity unit, (I was very big and they told me I had a big baby, so they didn't want me to go past my due date). At around 5 am I gave a big push and our lovely baby Lorna was born – not very big – she was only 7lb 14 oz. The most exciting time of our lives! We were involved in a House Church from that day on, as most of the young people, as well as the Pastor, left the Tabernacle, and a new church was born too.

Lorna Ruth

Jim's last bit

During all the time I'd lived in Liverpool, mum had lived close by to where John and Grace lived after they married, but now they had plans to move to another house, so we thought it would be good if mum came up to live in Liverpool to be with me. She came in August 1973 and initially had a room in the church house. She really enjoyed being in the house with me and being able to help out in the kitchen which was always a busy place. I think she was here in Liverpool for about six months and felt very much at home in the church fellowship.
Later that year, it finally happened ! One summer evening I had to go over to see a lady affectionately known in the church as Auntie May. As I was leaving, her niece called in to see her. Her name was Jean, yes, the one I had given a lift to when I began working at the church three years before. She had been coming to the church for some time, so I did already know her, but on this occasion, she somehow caught my eye and more importantly, my heart. Shortly after this I had to go to Wales on some business and asked her to come with me. I found we got on very naturally together and it wasn't long before our friendship grew into love and we started courting. As Jean was a nurse, she got her days off at varying times of the week, so when I could arrange the same day off we were able to go out on trips to the Wirral or Wales together. The only problem was that I sometimes didn't have any money, so she had to pay for petrol etc. to go on these trips!
It was nice that mum was here in Liverpool and got to see me start courting and gave her seal of approval when she said to Jean one day that she really liked her.

Sadly, on the 31 December of that year, mum had a major stroke and was rushed to hospital. She was unable to speak or walk. The hospital was not far from the church house, so I was able to go in every day to visit her. The nurses were very kind to her and allowed me in at any time – they asked me if I had a season ticket because I was there so much. Jean also came in often to do her hair for her (she had been a hairdresser before her nursing career).

Grace also came up regularly and after a few weeks, John and Grace came up together with their little girl Lorna to stay while Jean and I had a few days away at a friend's house in Scotland. While we were there, we went to visit some of my uncles and aunts who I hadn't seen for some years, and I introduced them to Jean and also showed Jean my birthplace. On the fourth day of our holiday, during a day out, we discussed our future and what we could do for mum, including whether we should get married and have her to come and stay with us so we could care for her. However, when we returned to the house where we were staying, we were given the sad news that my mum had passed away with a heart attack. Though I was very upset at this, we had to agree that she was ready to go home to heaven to be with her Lord, whom she loved and had served all her life. It was agreed that we should start back for Liverpool that evening, and our lovely friend David Wetherley who was also up there at that time agreed to come back with us. Mum's funeral was on 6th February 1974, it would have been her birthday on the 9th, when she would have been 68.

Grace writes of this time

  At that time in Birmingham, our fellowship had been getting too big for us to meet in our houses any more, and someone found the big house in Edgbaston Road, near Cannon Hill Park - where there were 7 flats going up for rent and the ground floor flat had this huge lounge. They decided that we lease the whole house and any families that wished to could move into the flats and the ground floor big lounge would be available for our meetings then.
 John's business partnership job with our friend Phil has just collapsed and he was out of work, so we decided to sell our house and move into one of the flats.
I was worried about moving away from Mum but thought maybe she could move into the one bedroom flat that was over the garage. Before I could mention it to her, she came round to see me the next morning, and during our conversation she said ' Do you know - I had a funny dream last night - I dreamt I went to live in Liverpool !' I asked her if she would like to do that and she replied that she wouldn't mind!'   Not long after was when you asked her to go up and live in the house and she was delighted!! I only wish we could have visited her more frequently!   But those were the days when we had very little spare money! I think John was working with a man from the fellowship making dolls houses'! - and got paid £25 per week.
When Mum was taken ill and you rang me to let me know, we had no money with which to buy petrol to come up to Liverpool the next morning. We had to pray - and in the morning we had a letter from (Dave and Mandy, I think) with a £10 note included! That week we spent in Liverpool while you were away in Scotland was very special for me - we would go to the hospital daily, with Lorna during the day, and sit and talk to her, then I would go on my own in the evenings. I don't know if I told you but on the last evening, while visiting her, the almoner called to chat with her and told me she was due to be released from hospital. I asked if she would improve, as she was still paralysed down the one side and couldn't speak. She just said 'there's every possibility'! I took that to mean 'Probably not'. So, I went back to see Mum for the rest of visiting

time, but feeling very sad!

When visiting time was finished I got up to leave and she pulled me very close and gave me a really tight long hug with the one arm that wasn't paralysed. She gave me a look that said "Sorry'. I left her, feeling very heartbroken for her situation. In the morning, just after breakfast, the hospital called, asking us to get there quickly as Mum had deteriorated.

We got there as quickly as we could, but she had gone!   It was a very emotional time - when they took us to see her, all I could think was 'She's not here - she's with the Lord!'   I also felt that she had asked the Lord to take her home - she couldn't bear the idea that she would be a burden to anyone in that situation she found herself in.

I was so grateful to have had the opportunity to spend that week in Liverpool, and taking Lorna and occasionally Paul (who I think was 3 months old at the time) to see her. While it was sad that you weren't there, I think the Lord was in that also - you were exhausted and in need of a rest.

It's wonderful to know that she is with the Lord, as our Dad is also! The years go by too quickly now, don't they? I can't believe I'll be 77 in July!!!!

Each day is a gift from God, isn't it?

Jimmy continues At the time of mums death

I had only been courting Jean for a few months, but she was such a comfort and encouragement to me at this time. In April, I proposed to her and we got engaged on the 25th of April. I didn't have any money to buy her a ring but just then my VW caravanette broke down and had to be scrapped and the church had a collection for me to get a new vehicle. I was given £250. With this money, I, first of all, bought an engagement ring for Jean for around £15 (she was worth a lot more than this, but she still managed to get the ring of her choice which she loved) and with the rest, I bought a minivan which got us back on the road.

Later that year I had to go to Italy for a month to do some work with a church in Udine and visit friends out there. I enjoyed the time there but was counting the days to coming back as I was missing Jean so much.

We set the date for our wedding, 18th January 1975. I'm not sure why we went for January, but the day turned out not too bad in the end, in fact, sunny and crisp. It was a lovely day for us despite the bin men coming to collect the bins while we were having the photos taken! They never came on a Saturday usually, but I think they quite enjoyed being in on our special day!

I had now finished working for the church and had a job in an electrical wholesaler which a friend from Church, Reg, managed to get me into, despite having no previous experience and we moved into a quaint little flat where 9 months later our lovely Jenny was born, the first of our three children. We've been married forty-four years now and have had many more adventures together while we have served the Lord, and we have much to be thankful for. Maybe sometime I will get the time and energy to write further of our exploits, adventures, family life and Gods faithfulnesses to us.

So, that's where we finish this part of the story of our lives together up until when we both married. Grace still lives in Birmingham with John, they have three children, two living in the Midlands and one in with his family on mission abroad and I am still living in Liverpool, retired, with Jean. Our three children live not far from us who are a joy and blessing to us.

I am writing the next episode now and it will be on Kindle, eventually!

Printed in Poland
by Amazon Fulfillment
Poland Sp. z o.o., Wrocław